A Practical Guide to the Commissioning Process

A Practical Guide to the Commissioning Process

Thomas Toftgaard Jarløv

2nd edition, 1st printing, 2023

A Practical Guide to the Commissioning Process

Publisher: Forlaget TTJ
2nd edition, 1st printing, 2023
ISBN 978-87-971885-3-8

Foreword

Commissioning is the answer to everything. That's what I learned from Ole Teisen, my mentor at Grontmij (now SWECO), a consulting firm. I've taken that with me to Copenhagen Airports A/S, the company that operates the Copenhagen Airport and Roskilde Airport. Here, with support from Niels Hunderup and other executives, I've implemented commissioning in every stage of our construction projects. This guide is an attempt at communicating my experience.

Thank you to my colleagues, Helene Anisimov, Jakob Søland Jensen, and René Borup Knorborg, for their review and input. Special thanks to Christian Molt Wengel at the Law Offices of Molt Wengel for guiding me through the legal aspects of commissioning.

Thank you to Copenhagen Airports A/S, my employer, for giving me the opportunity to experiment with and develop the commissioning process since 2015.

Last, but not least, thanks to my father and grandfather for their support. Their engagement in making this book a reality has been invaluable.

Thomas Toftgaard Jarløv, 2021

In 2015 Thomas launched our commissioning division at Copenhagen Airports A/S. Today, commissioning is in use for all of our larger construction projects. Commissioning has become a requirement for these larger projects because we've observed a significant difference in the number of errors and defects, as well as in handing off the technical systems to our operations division.

For us, it's important that the commissioning process be carried out in close collaboration with our project managers. This ensures good cross-disciplinary and cross-organisational coordination in our projects. Construction projects have many stakeholders, and the commissioning process is important in facilitating coordination between them - for internal and external parties alike.

Commissioning is often seen as "the owner's process", which it ultimately is, since we're the ones paying for it. However, our goal is for the process to be just as valuable to our external partners as it is to us. Because of that, we also see the commissioning process as a support process. It needs to help and support each of the parties involved in our construction projects to meet our requirements.

There is a global need to increase the use of sustainable solutions and minimise energy consumption in the future. The commissioning process is a great tool in this context, since it can be used to optimise and verify our energy consumption. Some of the ways we do this include focusing on sustainability when evaluating project materials, testing technical installations, and conducting ongoing monitoring of energy consumption in our buildings.

We have a clear goal of implementing commissioning for all of our construction projects in the future.

Christian Poulsen
Vice President, Technical Director, CTO, and CIO
Copenhagen Airports A/S

Table of contents

1. Introduction

The commissioning process is a quality management process that verifies and documents that a construction meets the Owner's requirements. The process is implemented right at the start of a construction project and runs throughout the project and into the operation of the construction. The commissioning process ensures that all interfaces among systems are functioning effectively and that technical installations are working according to the Owners requirements, as well as optimizing cooperation between the construction parties.

This guide describes how to carry out the activities of the commissioning process. The methods and tools described ensure that all commissioning activities described in the American Guideline, *ASHRAE Guideline 0-2019*, the American Standard for commissioning, *ASHRAE Standard 202-2018,* and the Danish Standard for commissioning, *DS 3090-2014,* are performed.

The guide also contains descriptions of commissioning tools that are based on experience from Copenhagen Airport's in-house commissioning process, as well as tools that are used in the Danish construction industry but are not included in standards and guidelines.

In addition to being a guide to commissioning, it is also useful as a control tool. The guide is therefore structured so that the sections can be used to determine commissioning services when entering into agreements with both the Design Team and the Contractor, as well as the commissioning provider. However, the guide cannot stand alone as a contract or agreement document, as the requirements and scope of the sections must be adapted to the current project.

Commissioning is the owner's tool for verifying a construction project. However, this guide is based on the assumption that all actors in a construction project must benefit from the commissioning process. If all project actors are to play an active role in the commissioning process, the process must make sense to all parties. This is ensured through commissioning, due to improved communication, the ability to manage technical installations and the prevention of errors and reduction in delays and wastage of resources.

The commissioning process is a support function that contributes to ensuring that building projects meet the Owner's requirements and specifications on completion.

The guide reviews concrete examples of how the tools of the commissioning process can be used and documented. The examples are structured as guidelines and based on concrete construction projects.

1.1. Purpose

There is still uncertainty in the construction industry as to how the individual commissioning activities are to be carried out. Consequently, commissioning processes are carried out that do not comply with the requirements of *ASHRAE Guideline 0, ASHRAE Standard 202* and *DS 3090*, and in some cases the Cx tools are also incorrectly used, so that the full benefits of the Cx process are not achieved.

This practical guide describes how to handle the individual commissioning activities and related documents in order to contribute to the development and standardization of the commissioning process.

There is a limited amount of documentation about how to perform the activities within the commissioning process. It can, therefore, be difficult to be educated or trained in commissioning. For this reason, another aim of the guide is to attract more people to take an interest in commissioning in practice.

The guide, therefore, provides concrete working methods, management tools and checklists that the Owner, as well as the commissioning team, can use to control what each commissioning activity includes at any time.

1.2. Scope

The guide includes all necessary commissioning activities to complete a commissioning process that complies with *ASHRAE Guideline 0, ASHRAE Standard 202* and *DS 3090*.

In addition, the guide contains commissioning tools that are used in the Danish construction industry but are not covered by any standards and guidelines. Each section also contains tips and tricks on how to best address the challenges you face during the commissioning process.

Overall, each section of the guide contains the following:

a. Process guidance on the planning and order of execution of commissioning activities.

b. Scope requirements specifying the content of commissioning activities.

c. Concrete descriptions and instructions on how commissioning activities are carried out.

1.3. Using the guide

Basic knowledge of construction processes and commissioning is an advantage. The guide can be used by commissioning teams, Owners, advisors, consultants, Design Teams and contractors, both when determining the scope and content of commissioning activities, and as a how-to description and management tool when commissioning activities are to be carried out.

The guide is split into sections according to the phases of a construction project and describes each commissioning activity during the associated phase. This means, for example, that the commissioning document, "Test overview" is described in two phases of the project: the general requirements for the content of the document are described in the Design Development section, where the document is drawn up, while the requirements for how to work with the document are described in the Construction Phase section.

The described tools and working methods can all be found in the commissioning software, www.CxPlanner.com. CxPlanner is a specialized commissioning application that can be used by all involved in construction projects to manage, document and perform commissioning.

2. Definitions and glossary

All the abbreviations and terms used in the guide are described below.

Acceptance document

contains the Owner's acceptance of a completed project phase and approval that the commissioning process must continue in the next phase.

APP Operating Requirements

the agreement document: "Additional conditions for operating requirements in construction (APP Operating Requirements)", edition 2018.

Basis of Design (BoD)

contains the Design Team's descriptions of how they have planned that the commissioning requirements are met in the project.

Best practices

is a specific approach that is recognized by a given industry as the best.

BMS

stands for "Building Management System" and is a control and management system for building installations. BMS is a monitoring and control system for buildings.

Commissioning (Cx)

is a general term for the commissioning process (see "commissioning process").

Commissioning activities (Cx Activities)

is the term for the works and activities covered by the Cx process.

Commissioning Design Review (Cx Design Review)

is the interdisciplinary review conducted by the Cx Team.

Commissioning documents (Cx documents)

is the term for the documents prepared in the Cx process.

Commissioning inspections (Cx inspections)

are the visual inspections that the Cx Team performs.

Commissioning Log (Cx Log)

contains all observations made/found during the entire commissioning process.

Commissioning Meeting (Cx Meeting)

are the specific commissioning meetings held by the Cx Team.

Commissioning organization (Cx Organization)

is the term for all the people who participate in the commissioning process. This includes the Cx Provider, Cx specialists, the Design Team, the Contractor, the builder, etc.

Commissioning Plan (Cx Plan)

contains the detailed plan of the commissioning activities on a construction project.

Commissioning process (Cx process)

is a quality management process that verifies and documents that a building complies with the Owner's requirements.

Commissioning Progress Reports (Cx Progress Reports)

are ongoing reports on the progress and status of Cx Activities compared to the progress of the project.

Commissioning Provider (Cx Provider)

is the chief executive of the commissioning process.

Commissioning Report (Cx Report)

is the final report that summarizes the commissioning process performed.

Commissioning service description (Cx service description)

is the contractual requirements for the Cx process used in entering into agreements.

Commissioning specialists (Cx specialists)

are members of the Cx Team who specialize in specific Cx Activities.

Commissioning team (Cx Team)

is the term for the people who are responsible for and carry out the commissioning activities. This includes the commissioning leader and the commissioning specialists.

Commissioning test (Cx test)

is the final interdisciplinary system integration test performed by the Cx Team (see SIT test).

Commissioning test period (Cx test period)

is the period during which the final Cx tests are performed.

Contractor

is the party with whom the Owner has entered into a legally binding agreement on the execution of all or parts of the construction.

Cost-benefit

is a calculation method for assessing whether a Cx process can pay off. The costs of the Cx process are compared with the savings achieved by the introduction of the Cx process.

Declaration of Conformity (DoC)

An EU declaration of conformity (DoC) is a mandatory document that you, as a manufacturer, or your authorized representative, need to sign to declare that your products comply with the EU requirements.

Design Team site inspection

persons employed by the adviser to carry out inspections. This can be, for example, visual inspection and review of operating and maintenance material.

Design Team

is the party responsible for designing the construction and often undertakes various project-related tasks.

Disc agreement

is an agreement that is entered into about the individual phases of the project.

DS 3090

is the abbreviation for the Danish standard for commissioning: "The commissioning process for buildings - Installations in new construction and major conversions".

Education plan

contains guidelines and descriptions of the teaching that must be carried out during and after the construction project, and which includes maintenance procedures.

FAT-test

stands for Factory Acceptance Test and includes testing of a system at the manufacturer's factory.

Handover

is when the building is taken into use for its intended purpose. For example, when users move in.

Load tests

are tests that require a specific load that can usually only be provided during the occupancy and operations phase; for example, by a given number of users using the building and the associated technical facilities.

Machinery Directive

The Machinery Directive sets requirements for machinery. It promotes harmonization through a combination of mandatory health and safety requirements and voluntary harmonized standards and it only applies to products that are to be placed on the EU market.

Machine manufacturer

is responsible for a machine system. In the case of assembled machines, one machine manufacturer is appointed who is responsible for the assembled machine system.

Monitoring Based Commissioning (MBCx)

are Cx Activities that are performed in the occupancy and operations phase, with the primary purpose of monitoring the construction.

Ongoing Cx

is the term for the commissioning process that continues into the occupancy and operations phase.

Operation and maintenance documentation (O&M documentation)

is the documentation that is used to be able to handle operation and maintenance of the building. These can be instructions for use, spare parts lists, emergency procedures, etc.

Owner's Project Requirements (OPR)

are the Owner's requirements for the construction, which the commissioning process must verify.

Phase approval

is acceptance of the completed project phase. The approval is made with the acceptance document.

Plant

is a technical installation that can function independently, for example a ventilation plant.

Pre-test

is the Contractor's system integration test (see SIT test).

Quality Assurance (QA)

is the quality assurance activities.

Review

is an analytical and structured review of a project material for compliance with defined requirements.

SAT-test

stands for "Site Acceptance Test" and includes testing of a plant when it is completed in construction.

Seasonal tests

are tests that require a specific season: summer or winter.

SIT-test

stands for "System Integrations Test" and an interdisciplinary system test that tests how several items work together and across contract and professional boundaries.

Site inspection

is a visual inspection of assembly.

System

are several items that work together, thereby together forming a system.

Systems Manual

describes the project's requirements for documentation.

Test overview

contains an overview of all plant in the project that are to be tested.

Test paradigms

contains the description of how a test should be performed.

Test reports

contains the reporting of tests and explains the relationship between the test results and the expected results.

Test schedule

is the detailed plan of when the various tests are to be performed and by whom.

Test

is verification by, for example, visual inspection, measurement or function testing.

Verification

is to prove the correctness or truth of something. In commissioning, it is verified that the construction complies with the commissioning requirements.

3. The Commissioning process

Commissioning is a quality-focused process that verifies, documents and tests that a building meets the Owner's Specified Requirements (OPR). The commissioning process is built around the commissioning requirements (OPR), which are measurable requirements developed at the start of a project. It is these requirements that are controlled and verified throughout all phases of the project - from the Pre-Design to the Occupancy and Operations Phase.

The commissioning process helps to plan, structure and ensure a continuous dialogue between the parties involved across the contracts and disciplines of the construction project, so that the Owner's requirements are verified at all stages of the project.

Technological developments have opened up new requirements for the integration and interconnection of technical installations in construction projects, making greater demands on the coordination between Design Team and Contractors and the respective disciplines and contracts. A continuous multidisciplinary focus across all installations throughout the project process is often needed to ensure proper system integration. Ensuring multidisciplinary focus and verifying system integration in theory and practice is one of the most important tasks of the commissioning process.

The commissioning process is not a replacement for existing works and processes in a building, but a complement. All project actors must still participate in the project and comply with the requirements of their agreements, even when commissioning is implemented.

3.1. Implementation

The commissioning process must be implemented already in the pre-design phase of the project, as it is at this stage that the commissioning requirements must be specified. It is in the early phases of a project that the choice of system structures is made and the requirements for system integration are specified. If errors or anomalies are discovered early in a project, it will be cheaper to correct them at this stage, rather than after the Construction Phase or in the Occupancy and Operations Phase.

An example may be that ventilation dampers controlled by a 4-20 mA signal have been selected, but that the BMS installation is designed with a control signal of 0-10 V. This will result in the BMS system not being able to control the ventilation dampers as expected. Such an error should be detected during the design phases and would then be significantly cheaper to correct, as only the project material needs to be modified.

If, on the other hand, the fault is first discovered during the Occupancy and Operations Phase, the cost and time consequences will be much greater if, for example, ceilings have to be dismantled in order to gain access to the ventilation dampers that are not working. In addition, areas of the building will not be available during the period when the fault is corrected.

Figure 1 illustrates the link between the ability to make changes to a project and the cost of making the changes, distributed over the phases of a project.

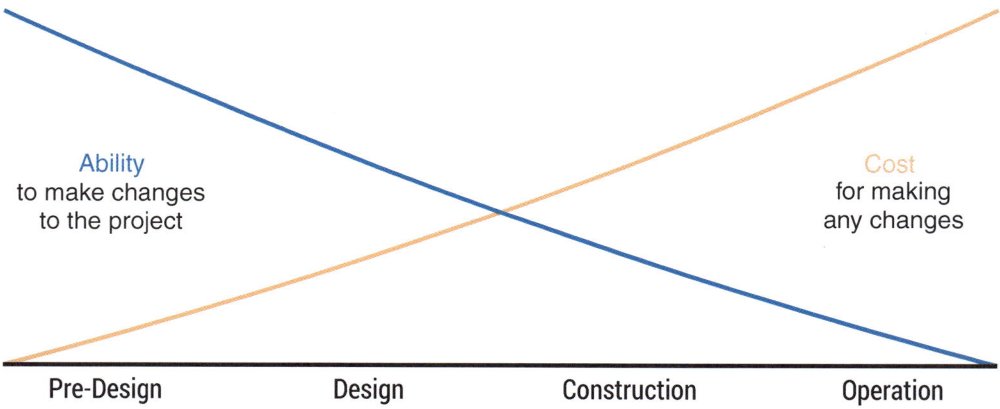

Figure 1. Project changes and cost over time in a project.

3.2. Scope of work

The extent of commissioning activities and the time that the commissioning team needs to solve them increases during the project. Figure 2 illustrates the expected workload compared to selected commissioning activities over time. The blue line illustrates the expected time spent.

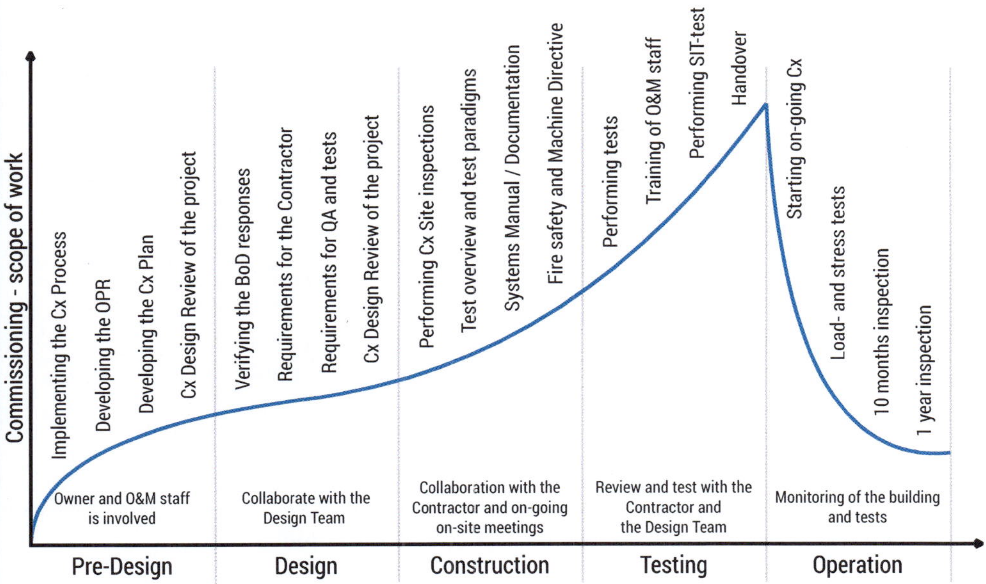

Figure 2. Commissioning tasks depicted relatively as resource consumption in relation to the time in the construction phase[1].

3.3. A support process

Commissioning is often referred to as the "Owner's process", as it is the Owner who pays and implements it, but the Design Team and Contractors in a project also greatly benefit from the process. The commissioning process is a tool and support function for all the actors in a project, as the aim is, among other things, to verify all interfaces between disciplines and contracts, thereby helping all actors in the project to comply with the commissioning requirements.

It is often seen in Danish construction projects that major Contractor companies that offer turnkey contracts have included their own commissioning process in the price. They implement commissioning because it makes the interfaces between the disciplines visible and documents that a building is delivered and it meets the Owner's Project Requirements. The Design Team or Contractor's own commissioning process does not replace the Owner's commissioning process, but it is a good complement and the two commissioning processes must be combined on a project-by-project basis.

[1] Inspiration to figure comes from "Værdibyg - Commissioning-processen, 2013"

3.4. Sustainability certificates

There are several sustainability certifications[2], which include the use of commissioning. By using commissioning, more "points" can be achieved, which can contribute to an improved score in the sustainability certification. Three of the widely used certifications which include commissioning are:

a. LEED published by "Leadership in Energy and Environmental Design".

b. BREEAM published by the "Building Research Establishment Environmental Assessment Method".

c. DGNB published by the "German Sustainable Building Council".

They all include elements of the commissioning process, including test paradigms, training of operating staff and 10 months' review. Using the specified tools and methods contained in this guide will ensure that the commissioning requirements of the 3 sustainability certifications are met.

3.5. Pricing

Commissioning costs are often calculated as a percentage between 0.5-2% of the total construction cost per building. However, this is only an indicative key figure, as commissioning costs depend on the complexity of the technical installations and the disciplines included in the commissioning process.

Cost-benefit analyses show that the use of commissioning is a financial advantage for the Owner, although commissioning is an additional service that the Owner must pay for. There are multiple cost-benefit analyses[3][4], all of which document that the savings resulting from commissioning exceed the cost of purchasing commissioning.

These analyses are primarily based on the Owner's direct savings, but often the Owner also experiences several indirect savings. These could be better indoor climate, adherence to deadlines or reduced energy usage.

[2] Sustainability certifications divide buildings into different categories depending on the sustainability of a building. There are several different certification schemes, all using different methodologies and calculation models for this categorization.

[3] Rúnar Örn Ágústsson: Advantages and disadvantages of the process (2010)

[4] Lawrence Berkeley National Laboratory: Building Commissioning Costs and Savings Across Three Decades and 1,500 North American Buildings (2020)

In addition to the Owner's savings, the Design Team and the Contractor often also experience savings, which results in fewer errors in delivery, fewer misunderstandings across interfaces and, in addition, there will be concrete evidence that the Owner's Project Requirements have been met. Operating staff will also have fewer problems and operational challenges in the post-takeover period.

Often the operating costs in terms of maintenance and energy costs of a building over time will exceed the construction costs of the building. Commissioning ensures optimization of operating routines, energy consumption, etc., which have an impact on operating costs. Figure 3 illustrates the Owner's operating costs for a normal building, compared to a building where commissioning has been used.

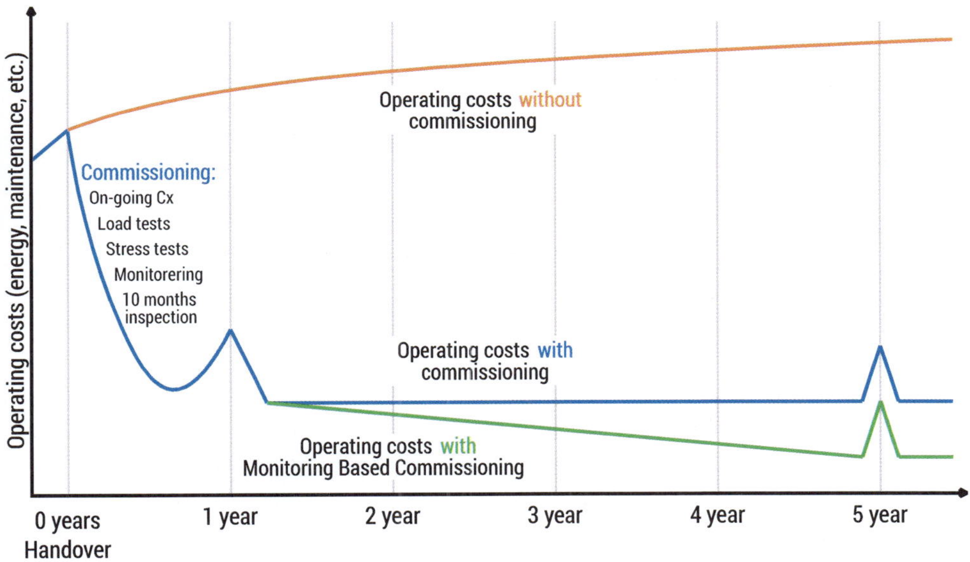

Figure 3. Operating costs using commissioning[5].

3.6. Independent commissioning provider

The commissioning process is led by the commissioning provider who, in cooperation with the commissioning team, is responsible for the commissioning activities being carried out. Persons participating in the commissioning team must have the appropriate level of competence and technical expertise to carry out cross-disciplinary verifications.

[5] Inspiration for the figure comes from "Værdibyg - Commissioning-processen, 2013"

The Owner must ensure that the commissioning provider is an independent third party who is not employed by or financially dependent on either the Design Team or the Contractor. This is a requirement in order to avoid impartiality problems, which could be, for example, that the commissioning team finds errors that are caused by the Contractor and can thus have an economic impact on the Contractor. In exceptional cases where it is not possible to hire an independent commissioning provider, a binding independent agreement must be drawn up.

3.7. Phases of the commissioning process

The commissioning process is divided into phases that follow the phases of a construction project. The commissioning phase model used must be adapted to the phase model of the current project. This guide is based on the construction phase model based on *ASHRAE Guideline 0*, *ASHRAE Standard 202* and *DS 3090*, which contains:

- Pre-Design
- Design Development
- Construction Documents
- Construction Phase
- Occupancy and Operations Phase

3.8. Process overview

The process overview in Figure 4 shows a sample of the commissioning activities described in this guide. The process overview is based on the phases of a construction project and the respective commissioning activities can be viewed during each phase.

The illustration is based on "best practices", where the commissioning process is an essential part of the project and runs through all stages of the project. If the Owner uses a different phase-model, the commissioning activities must be moved and divided to suit it.

The grey boxes in Figure 4 symbolize commissioning activities, each described in this guide. The light blue boxes in the illustration show which project phase the grey boxes belong to.

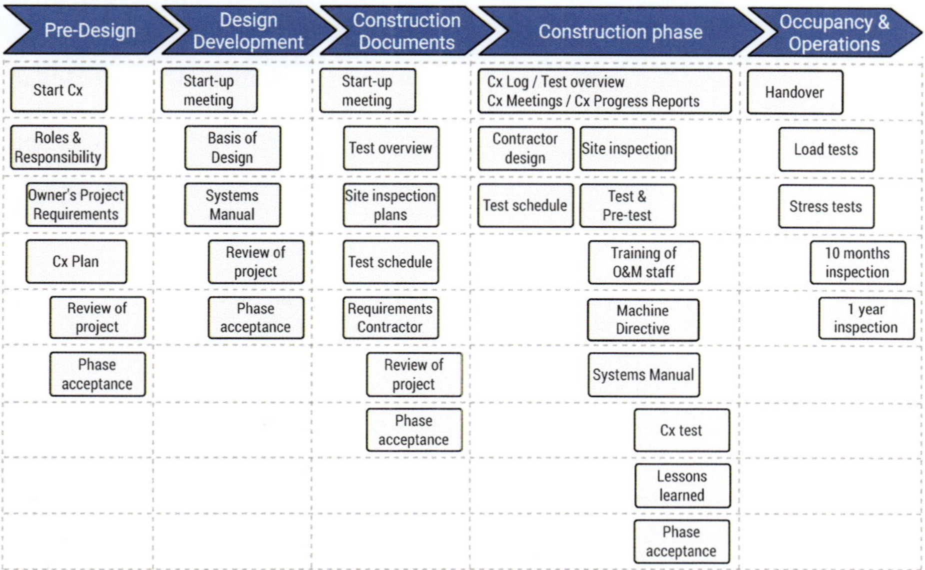

Figure 4. Commissioning activities distributed in their phases.

4. Standards and guidelines

There are a whole series of standards and guidelines describing how the commissioning process should be carried out. The approach, level of detail and process of these documents varies, depending on the country of publication. This guide is based on the recognized standard and guideline *ASHRAE Standard 202* and *ASHRAE Guideline 0*; and the *Danish Standard DS 3090*.

Common to the three documents is that they all describe Cx as a process. This means that Cx is implemented at the start of the project and runs through the entire project.

Each section of this guide contains a table indicating whether the section is covered by the above standards and guideline.

4.1. ASHRAE Standard 202

ASHRAE (American Society of Heating, Refrigerating and Air-Conditioning Engineers)[6] has published a Cx standard that is used and referenced globally.

The definition of commissioning in ASHRAE Standard 202:

> The Commissioning Process (Cx) is a quality-focused process for enhancing the delivery of a project. Cx focuses on evaluating and documenting that all of the commissioned systems and assemblies are planned, designed, installed, tested, operated, and maintained to meet the Owner's Project Requirements (OPR).
>
> — ASHRAE Standard 202

4.1.1. Changes from this guide

This guide contains more requirements and recommendations for the Cx Process than those described in *ASHRAE Standard 202*, *ASHRAE Guideline 0* and *DS 3090*. These include tools which ensures better governance and cooperation in the Cx Process:

[6] ASHRAE - https://www.ashrae.org/

a. Start-up meetings with the Design Team and the Contractor
b. Test overview
c. Test schedule
d. Cx progress report
e. Cx Meetings
f. Machinery Directive
g. Pre-test
h. Entry into service
i. Cost-benefit

4.1.2. Structure of ASHRAE Standard 202

The standard is structured over the individual Cx Activities and their annexes:

1. Start of the Cx process
2. OPR
3. Cx Plan
4. Basis of Design (BoD)
5. Requirements for the Design Team and the Contractor
6. Review
7. Test
8. Systems Manual
9. Training
10. Operational activities
11. Cx Report

4.2. ASHRAE Guideline 0

ASHRAE Guideline 0 is built around the phases of a construction project. In each phase description, the requirements for the individual Cx Activities are described. The Guideline also contains 18 appendix describing working methods and examples of the documents.

The definition of commissioning in ASHRAE Guideline 0:

> The Commissioning Process (Cx) is a quality-focused process for enhancing the delivery of a project by achieving, validating, and documenting the performance of facility elements in meeting the objectives and criteria of the Owner. Cx extends through all phases of new or major renovation projects, from predesign to Owner occupancy and operation, with tasks during each phase to ensure verification of design, construction, and operator training.
>
> — ASHRAE Guideline 0

4.2.1. Changes from this guide

The changes described in section 4.1.1, “Changes from this guide” also apply to *ASHRAE Guideline 0*.

4.2.2. Structure of ASHRAE Guideline 0

This guideline is structured over the project phases:

a. Pre-design Phase

b. Design Phase

c. Construction Phase

d. Occupancy/Occupation Phase

e. Appendix

4.3. Danish Standard DS 3090

In Denmark, it is the Danish standard *DS 3090* that sets the tone for how Cx should be performed. The standard has helped to define how Cx is carried out in the Danish construction industry.

The standard contains descriptions of the required Cx Activities and the 11 required Cx Documents. Process recommendations for the Cx Activities are described, but the standard does not contain specific scope and execution descriptions.

Sometimes Owner's include the standard in its entirety in tender documents without adapting it to the current project. This entails the risk that tenders will not submit tenders documents on the same basis. Likewise, there is a risk that the Cx Process does not meet the Owner's expectations. Therefore, the standard **must** always be adapted to the current project.

The definition of commissioning in DS 3090[7]:

> The commissioning process for buildings is a quality-focused process that is carried out to obtain, verify and document that a building's facilities, installations and systems are planned, projected, installed and tested, as well as being serviced and maintained to meet the requirements of total costs, building regulations and other legislation, as well as the Owner's clearly defined requirements. As a result, the commissioning process will continue throughout the lifetime of the construction, so that operating staff continuously follow up on compliance with commissioning requirements.
>
> — Dansk Standard DS 3090

4.3.1. Changes from this guide

The changes described in section 4.1.1, "Changes from this guide" also apply to *DS 3090*.

[7] Quoting DS 3090 is approved by Dansk Standard.

This is partly because, since the release of *DS 3090* in 2014, updated contract documents and service descriptions have been published in the Danish construction industry.

One of the main changes is that the project phases over which the Cx Process is built have changed their name since the release of *DS 3090*. The old term "Main project" has been replaced by "Tender project"[8] in *YBL18*. This guide is based on the new designations for the project phases.

4.3.2. Structure of DS 3090

DS 3090 is divided into the following main topics:

a. Organization
b. Documents of the Cx process
c. Cx Activities
    a. Idea and programming
    b. Outline and project proposals *(Proposals phase)*
    c. Main Project *(Tender Project Phase)*
    d. Construction Phase *(Execution phase)*
    e. Operational phase
d. Annex

In order to comply with the standard, 11 documents must be drawn up. It must be possible to save all the documents as separate documents.

1. Cx Requirements Document (OPR)
2. Cx Plan
3. Cx Log
4. Acceptance document (phase approval)
5. Basis of Design (BoD)
6. Cx Design Review report

[8] Tender project can form the basis for tender, preparation of execution project and execution.

7. Training plan
8. Test paradigms
9. Test reports
10. Systems Manual
11. Cx Report

5. Pre-Design phase

The Pre-Design phase includes the Owner's requirements, expectations and wishes for the final construction. These requirements are summarized in Pre-Design documents which constitute the project material.

The Cx requirements must be incorporated into the Pre-Design documents at this stage to ensure that they become an integral part of them. In addition to the specific Cx requirements, the Pre-Design must contain the Owner's Project Requirements for commissioning and testing. The Cx Team must therefore, ensure that the requirements are consistent with the planned Cx Process.

FIDIC defines the "Pre-Design" as:

Pre-Design

> This phase generally needs to be iterative with the process of land acquisition
>
> — FIDIC, Definition of Services Guidelines (Civil Works) 2016

The Pre-Design will constitute the first project material offered to a Design Team, who will prepare the project material in the next phase.

5.1. Commissioning activities

Activity	Document	Description
Implement Cx	Agreement and contract	The Cx process is implemented in contracts, and the Cx Provider draws up a budget for the Cx process to the Owner.
Build Cx-organization	Organization chart	The participants in the Cx Organization are designated. The Cx Organization is continuously adapted to the projects needs.
Arrange start-up meeting	Meeting agenda & minutes	Hold a start-up meeting with the Design Team, where the Cx Activities are reviewed.
Develop the OPR items	OPR	The OPR items are developed with the Owner's O&M staff. The final OPR is approved by the Owner.
Plan the Cx Activities	Cx Plan	The Cx Process is described in the Cx Plan. The Cx Plan will be updated with details during the project.
Start the Cx Log	Cx Log	The Cx Log is created and all participants in the project get access to it. Cx observations are added to it during the project.

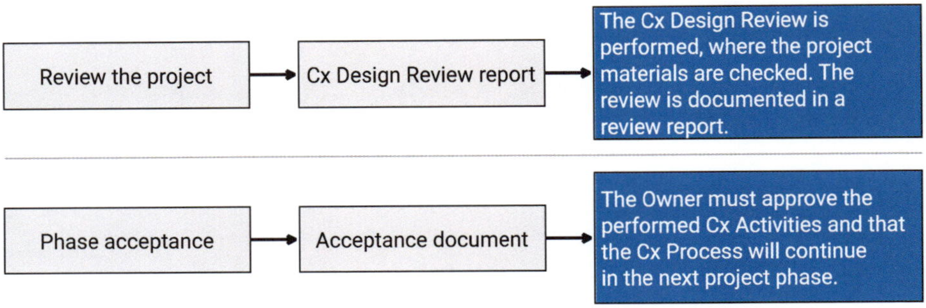
Review the project
Cx Design Review report
The Cx Design Review is performed, where the project materials are checked. The review is documented in a review report.
Phase acceptance
Acceptance document
The Owner must approve the performed Cx Activities and that the Cx Process will continue in the next project phase.

5.2. Roles and responsibility

Requirements from	Perform activity	Prepare document
ASHRAE G0	**Required**	**Required**
ASHRAE STD 202	**Required**	Not required
DS 3090	**Required**	**Required**

Throughout the Cx process, there must be clarity as to who is responsible for the Cx Activities. It is the Cx Provider who has overall responsibility for defining the roles and responsibilities of all Cx Participants.

5.2.1. The Commissioning Provider

Responsibility for leading the Cx process must be defined and assigned at the beginning of the Pre-Design phase. The person entrusted with overall responsibility for the Cx process will be referred to as the Cx Provider. However, the Owner will be responsible for the Cx process at all times.

The Cx Provider is responsible for managing and ensuring that all Cx Activities are performed. However, it is common management practice for the Cx Provider to delegate responsibility for the implementation of the individual Cx Activities to the participants in the Cx Team. Where responsibility for an activity is delegated, this must be explicitly described in the Cx Plan.

The selected Cx Provider must have the necessary skills and experience to manage a Cx process. An assessment of the qualifications of potential candidates must include the following elements:

a. Experience with the management and execution of Cx Activities from other projects (management of the Cx Log, preparation of multidisciplinary tests, etc.).

b. Cx certifications (e.g. CMCP, QCxP, CxA, CxM, etc.)[9].

c. Competences in site inspection and a technical background.

The Cx Provider must not participate in the design or execution of the construction or be employed by the Design Team or Contractor's company, as this may entail a risk of ineligibility.

[9] Building Commissioning Professional (BCxP, ASHRAE), Qualified Commissioning Process Provider (QCxP, WISC), Accredited Commissioning Process Authority Professional (CxAP, WISC), Accredited Commissioning Process Manager (CxM, WISC)

In cases where this cannot be complied with, an agreement must be drawn up describing how this is handled.

5.2.2. The Commissioning team

The Cx Team is the definition of those who work exclusively with Cx Activities. This includes the execution, management and documentation of the Cx Activities. The Cx Team consists of the Cx Provider and Cx specialists.

The Cx Team must be formed already in the Pre-Design phase. However, throughout the project, the Cx Team will be continuously modified and adapted to ensure that there are competent Cx specialists with the necessary professional competencies at all times. Therefore, when new technical disciplines are included in the project, the Cx Team will need to be expanded to include Cx specialists who have the necessary skills in these areas.

Participants in the Cx Team must not participate in the design or execution of the construction or be employed by the Design Team or Contractor's company, as this may entail a risk of ineligibility.

In cases where this cannot be complied with, an agreement must be drawn up describing how this is handled.

Usually both the Cx Provider and Cx specialists come from the same company.

5.2.3. The Commissioning organization

The Cx Organization is the name of all the parties involved in the Cx process. This often includes:

a. Cx Provider

b. Cx Specialists

c. The representative of the Owner (the representative appointed by the Owner can be, for example, the operating staff or the end user)

d. The Owner's advisor

e. The Project Manager

f. The Design Manager

g. The Construction Manager

h. The Design Team's Cx specialists

i. The Contractor's Cx specialists

The Cx Provider and the Owner are responsible for appointing the specialists to participate in the Cx Organization; however, in some situations, the Owner may choose to assign this responsibility to the Cx Provider.

Participants in the Cx Organization must be authorized to take binding decisions on behalf of the company they represent.

5.2.4. Communication flow

The communication flow to and from the Cx Organization must be clearly defined so that the right persons receive the relevant information and documents. Usually the Cx Provider will be the primary recipient, as the Cx Provider has overall responsibility for managing the planning of the Cx Process and for continuously communicating with the Owner.

As the Cx Organization expands, the Cx Provider must update the communication flow and communicate any changes. For large projects with many participants, it is recommended that the Cx Provider delegates the primary communication responsibility for selected Cx Activities; for example, for each item in the Cx Log, a responsible party may be designated to ensure all communication around the individual item.

The communication flow must be defined as part of the Cx Plan and must specify at least who is the recipient and sender of:

a. Inquiries to the Cx Organization.

b. Cx minutes of meetings.

c. Updates to the Cx Log.

d. Updates to the Cx Plan.

e. The follow-up on Cx Design Review reports.

f. Amendments and deviations to the OPR.

Basic decisions, such as the subject area on emails and file naming, must be decided in the project organization. If no file-sharing system is used, there must be a clear naming procedure for files.

File names must be constructed with a date indication at the beginning, file description and then revision/version number. The date entry must be formatted as ”YYYY-MM-DD” for the purpose of sorting the documents in chronological order, for example ”2019-12-01 - Filename_v1.0.pdf”. For more requirements for file naming, see section 6.4, “Systems Manual”.

5.2.5. Example of communication flow

Activity/Document	Description	Recipients
Review	1) Receive the project material. 2) Submission of Cx Design Review reports. 3) Receive the Design Team's reply to the review report.	1) Cx Provider 2) Design Team 3) Cx Provider
Cx Inspection	Receive Cx Inspection notes.	Cx Team Construction Manager
Test overview	1) Receive updates to installations in the Test overview, e.g. completed TAB. 2) Submission of updates.	1) Cx Provider 2) Cx Provider
Phase acceptance	Phase Approval Documents.	Owner
Cx Plan	Updates to the Cx Plan.	Cx Organization Owner

Table 1. Example of communication flow for Cx Activities.

Document	Frequency	Recipients
Cx Log	1/week	Cx Team
Cx Meeting Minutes	On update	Cx Team Owner Construction Manager
Test overview	On update	Cx Team
Test reports	On update	Cx Team Contractor
Cx Meeting Minutes	On update	Cx Team Owner

Table 2. Example of communication flow for Cx documents.

5.2.6. Activity Matrix

An activity matrix can be used to specify who is responsible for performing tasks and who can approve deliveries from specific tasks. An activity matrix is often divided into 4 main roles:

- **Input from** = Who has important knowledge and has to contribute information.
- **Performs** = Who is responsible for performing the task.
- **Approver** = Who can take decisions and be held responsible for execution.
- **Used by** = Who needs the delivery from the task.

In order to make roles and responsibilities visible in the Cx process, an activity matrix can be drawn up that contains all the tasks in the Cx process. By using an activity matrix, it is made clear who is responsible for performing the individual Cx Activities. See section 10.1, “Cx Activity Matrix” for an example.

5.2.7. Organization chart

It is necessary to produce an organizational chart of the participants in the Cx process that is accessible to all. The diagram must at least show who is to participate in the Cx Organization and may be supplemented by indicating who has authority for different decision-making. Figure 5 shows an example of a Cx organization chart illustrating all the parties that are part of the Cx organization.

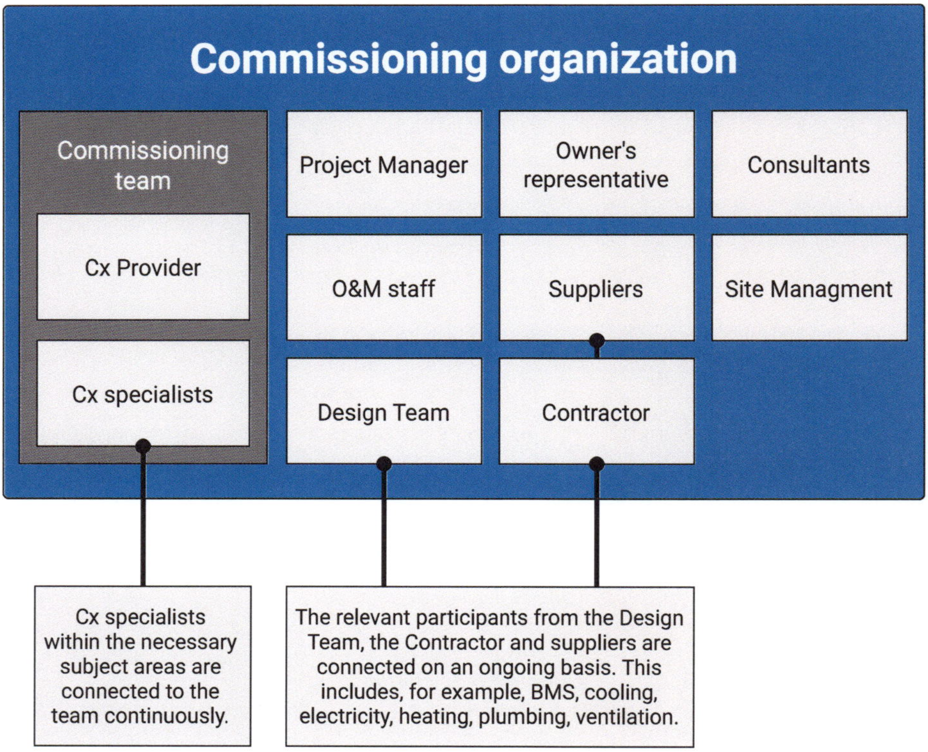

Figure 5. Example of a Cx organization chart.

5.3. Cost overview

Requirements from	Perform activity	Prepare document
ASHRAE G0	**Required**	**Required**
ASHRAE STD 202	Not required	Not required
DS 3090	Not required	Not required

The costs of the Cx process must be related to the scope and complexity of the OPR in conjunction with the level of detail of the Cx Plan.

5.3.1. Fixed price

It may be difficult to specify a fixed price for the Cx process, as the workload is often directly related to the number of errors found in the project material and during execution. Therefore, the Owner must also be in agreement that, if there are many errors during the Cx process, and the Cx Team shall follow up and try to fix them, this may require an increase in the budget.

In the event of a fixed price, the Cx Provider should clearly detail in the Cx contract documents how to deal with unforeseen errors found during the Cx Process.

5.3.2. Cost per Cx Activity

The Cx Provider can use a "Cost per Cx Activity"-scheme to calculate the costs of the Cx process. The scheme must include an estimate of the number of hours expected to be spent on the Cx process by the Cx Provider, the Cx Team, the Design Team and the Contractor.

The estimate can also be used to check that the Design Team and Contractor have set aside sufficient time for participation in the Cx Activities in their offers.

If an activity matrix has been prepared, it can often form the structure of the "Cost per Cx Activity"-schema. See section 5.2.6, “Activity Matrix” for information about the Activity Matrix.

Figure 6 shows how a "Cost per Cx Activity"-scheme can be built up during the Pre-Design phase. For each Cx Activity, the number of hours expected to be spent by each party is indicated.

Cx Activity	Cx Provider	Cx Team	Design Team	Contractor	Owner
Price estimate	10	0	0	0	5
Scope of the Cx Process	5	0	0	0	5
OPR	20	50	10	0	15
Cx Plan	15	0	0	0	0
Start-up meeting	5	5	0	0	5
Cx Log	10	0	0	0	0
Cx Design Review	10	75	20	0	15
Phase acceptance	5	0	0	0	2

Figure 6. Cost per Cx Activity for the Pre-Design phase. For each Cx Activity, the number of hours expected to be spent by each party is indicated.

5.3.3. Documented usage of cost in Cx Progress Reports

For the ongoing Cx Progress Reports (see section 8.4, “Commissioning Progress Reports”), the Cx Provider can use the "Cost per Cx Activity" schema. Cx Progress Reports document the progress of the various Cx Activities; therefore, the Cx Provider will be able to show the Owner early in the process if additional hours are required.

5.4. Scope of commissioning process

Requirements from	Perform activity	Prepare document
ASHRAE G0	Not required	Not required
ASHRAE STD 202	Not required	Not required
DS 3090	**Required**	**Required**

The scope of the Cx process is often based on the OPR and the technical installations covered by this. The scope has a direct impact on how much time the Cx Team needs for verification, which also affects the costs of Cx.

5.4.1. Required scope

ASHRAE G0 requires the following items to be in the scope:

a. Project schedule and budget.

b. Cx scope and budget.

c. Project documentation requirements, including format for submittals, training materials, reports, and the Systems Manual. Consideration should be given to use of electronic format documents and records where appropriate.

d. Owner directives.

e. Restrictions and limitations.

f. User requirements.

g. Occupancy requirements and schedules.

h. Training requirements for Owner's personnel.

i. Warranty requirements.

j. Benchmarking requirements.

k. O&M criteria for the facility that reflect the Owner's expectations and capabilities and the realities of the facility type.

l. Equipment and system maintainability expectations, including limitations of O&M personnel.

m. Quality requirements for materials and construction.
n. Allowable tolerance in facility system operations.
o. Energy efficiency goals.
p. Environmental and sustainability goals.
q. Community requirements.
r. Adaptability for future facility changes and expansion.
s. Systems integration requirements, especially across disciplines.
t. Health, hygiene, and indoor environment requirements.
u. Acoustical requirements.
v. Vibration requirements.
w. Seismic requirements.
x. Accessibility requirements.
y. Security requirements.
z. Aesthetics requirements.
aa. Constructability requirements.
ab. Communication requirements.
ac. Applicable codes and standards.

ASHRAE STD 202 has fewer items as the required scope:

a. Facility objectives, size, location, user requirements, and Owner directives
b. Environmental, sustainability, and efficiency goals and benchmarks
c. Indoor environment requirements, including temperature, humidity, and ventilation
d. Space use and occupancy and operations schedules
e. Clearly defined Cx scope and requirements
f. Equipment, systems and assemblies requirements, expectations, and warranty provisions
g. Maintainability, access, and operational performance requirements

h. Installation evaluation and testing requirements
i. Project documentation, Cx Progress Reports, Systems Manual requirements and formats
j. Training requirements for Owner's operations and maintenance (O&M) personnel, emergency response personnel, and occupants, including level of training required, qualifications of trainers, and documentation requirements
k. Designer Basis of Design (BoD) milestone submission requirements
l. Applicable codes and standards in addition to local building codes
m. Project schedules
n. Special project requirements
o. The content, organization, and milestones of BoD submittals for the design and construction process
p. The number, format, and scheduling of design and submittal reviews
q. Sampling procedures, if permitted, for all reviews, evaluations, and testing
r. Cx Progress Report formats and distributed intervals

DS 3090 has another approach, where by the scope is defined based on specific technical installations:

a. Lighting installations (including daylight management and solar shading)
b. Fire ventilation
c. Fire alarm systems
d. Building Management System (BMS)
e. Electrical installations
f. Supply systems (heat pumps, district heating supply, groundwater cooling)
g. Cooling systems
h. Indoor climate
i. Heating systems
j. Ventilation systems
k. Other supply systems

5.4.2. Technical installations

Besides the required scope, the Cx Provider must clarify with the Owner whether the Cx process should also include the building's fire safety installations. If the fire safety installations do not work correctly, it will not be possible to put the building into service. Fire safety installations include:

a. Acoustic Warning System
b. Automatic Fire Alarm System
c. Automatic Fire Extinguisher
d. Automatic Fire Sprinkler System
e. Automatic Fire Ventilation
f. Power-Operated Fire Doors

In addition, other business-critical installations and operationally heavy installations may be included:

a. Automatic doors (carousel doors, sliding door, wind trap, etc.)
b. Elevators
c. Ozone/UV installations
d. Roller pavements
e. Escalators
f. IT Server installations
g. Access control

5.4.3. Scope of commissioning activities

If some Cx Activities are discarded, the process cannot, in principle, be described as a Cx process. However, there may be cases where individual Cx Activities are already dealt with in another way in the construction project, which is why they can be waived. This could, for example, be the Basis of Design, if specialist meetings are held at which the Design Team describes how the items in the OPR are implemented.

There may also be cases where it is not possible to include all the Cx Activities in a project. This may be due to the Owner's finances or if the Owner's project process does not allow the implementation of certain Cx Activities. In such cases, the Cx Provider must make concrete proposals to the Owner on how the Cx process can be optimized by merging selected Cx Activities with existing work in the construction project, for example by combining the Design Team's site inspections with the Cx Site Inspections. In addition, the optimization proposals should also include the use of the Owner's own resources for carrying out Cx Activities and similar optimization proposals.

If only a few Cx Activities are implemented, such as testing, it cannot and must not be referred to as a Cx process. Cx is dependent on it being a process that runs from the Pre-Design into the Operation phase. If there are some Cx Activities that are not implemented, there is a risk that the requirements in *ASHRAE G0*, *ASHRAE STD 202* and *DS 3090* will not be met and that the expected value of the Cx process will not be achieved.

If Cx Activities are deviated from, an impact assessment must be carried out that assesses the impact of the deviation and whether there are possible mitigating actions. For example, if it is not possible to implement the Basis of Design, the Cx Team may organize professional coordination meetings with the Design Team, where they match expectations and solutions for the OPR. This is not an optimal solution, however, and should only be used unless there is no alternative.

5.5. Start-up meeting with the Design Team

Requirements from	Perform activity	Prepare document
ASHRAE G0	Not required	Not required
ASHRAE STD 202	Not required	Not required
DS 3090	Not required	Not required

Once the Design Team for the Pre-Design phase has been selected, a start-up meeting must be held to review all planned and anticipated Cx Activities in the current project phase. The purpose of the meeting is to ensure a match with the expectations of the persons from the Design Team who will participate in the Cx Team.

The Cx Provider is responsible for convening and holding the start-up meeting and documenting that it has been held. The Design Team will be contractually obliged to attend the meeting.

5.5.1. Meeting structure

Before the meeting, the Cx Provider must submit a project-specific agenda for the meeting to the Design Team. The agenda will contain at least:

a. Time and place.

b. Introduction to the Cx process.

c. Communication flow, responsibilities and roles.

d. The Design Team's involvement in the Cx process.

e. The Design Team's responsibilities and deliveries.

f. The Contractor's expected involvement in the Cx process.

5.5.2. Example of detailed agenda

Time / Place	12:00-15:00 / Meeting room 8
Phase	Pre-Design
Cx Provider	Thomas Toftgaard Jarløv
Participants	a) Jens Jensen b) Hans Hansen c) Ole Olesen
1) Communication flow	a) Creating a mailing list for information b) Single-Point-Of-Contact c) Documentation flow d) Information flow
2) Roles & Responsibility	a) The Owner's and Cx Providers interfaces b) Opportunities to change project material, schedules and handover
3) Design Teams involvement	Design Teams responsibility and deliverables a) Participation in developing the OPR b) Input to the Cx Plan c) Input to the Cx Log d) Compliance with the requirements of the Cx Design Review e) Phase evaluation
4) The Contractor's expected involvement in the Cx Process	The attached Cx plan for the upcoming project phases forms the basis for the Contractor's involvement.
5) Other	a) Risks and interfaces b) Questions c) Next meeting

Figure 7. Agenda for the start-up meeting with the Design Team.

5.6. Owner's Project Requirements

Requirements from	Perform activity	Prepare document
ASHRAE G0	**Required**	**Required**
ASHRAE STD 202	**Required**	**Required**
DS 3090	**Required**	**Required**

The Cx process is built around the Owner's Project Requirements (OPR), which are verified in all phases of the project; therefore, the OPR must be developed already in the Pre-Design phase. An efficient and value-adding Cx process depends on clear and measurable items in the OPR. The requirements must be formulated and structured in such a way that, when verified, no one may be in doubt as to whether the requirements are complied with.

The OPR also ensures that the Design Team and Contractor know what the Owner expects and wants. The Design Team will, therefore, be in a position to prepare detailed project material that meets the Owner's wishes, and the Contractor will be better able to price the project, as there is no doubt about the outcome requirements. Together, it ensures a reconciliation of expectations across the construction parties, while at the same time giving the Owner a true and fair view of the overall project economy.

5.6.1. Scope of the OPR

The OPR helps to define the scope of the Cx process. The number of requirements in the OPR and the content of the requirements define which areas the Cx process should cover and the amount of the Cx Team needs to perform. There must be a direct link between the OPR and the specified scope of the Cx process (see section 5.4, "Scope of commissioning process"). The requirements must be adapted to each project based on the Owner's wishes and expectations for the project in conjunction with:

a. Criticality

b. Complexity

c. Cost

Often the Owner specifies requirements that focus on areas which the Owner has experienced challenges with in the past. In addition to the requirements covering these areas, it is the responsibility of the Cx Team to the Owner to define project-specific requirements for interfaces that would not otherwise be covered.

In addition to the Owner's requirements, the OPR must also include:

a. Documentation requirements (flow, verification and delivery requirements for As-Built, QA, O&M and tests).

b. Requirements for testing technical installations (verification of functionality of installations).

c. Requirements for the timing and period of test activities.

d. Requirements for the training of O&M staff.

e. Requirements for maintenance, energy consumption and sustainability.

5.6.2. Verifiable requirements

An item in the OPR must be verifiable; therefore, it must be formulated using measurable parameters. Measurable parameters are fixed and their wording or outcome must not be open to interpretation. When defined with measurable parameters, the requirements will also indirectly help to ensure that the requirement can be read independently and thus constitute an expectation match.

The Cx requirements must therefore not contain words such as: "reasonable, sufficient, should be experienced, felt, easy". There may be situations where these words can be allowed, but it must then be ensured that they are only used in conjunction with a fixed measurable parameter.

Example A1 below indicates that "... the operating staff can easily access them." which does not contain a measurable parameter. Both the Design Team and the Contractor will be able to interpret what the outcome is, as the concept of "easy access" is a subjective assessment. Example A2 below shows how the requirement could be formulated in this case:

> **Example A1 (not approved OPR item):**
> All measuring outlets in the cooling unit must be located so that the operating staff can easily access them.

> **Example A2 (approved OPR item):**
> All measuring outlets in the cooling unit must be accessible without aids and have a maximum height above the floor of 1.8 meters.

Example B1 below indicates "... possibility to get an overview ...", which does not contain a measurable parameter. The possibility of *something* will always be a relative view, as the Design Team, Contractor and Owner may have different views on this. Example B2 below shows how this case (B1) could be formulated:

> **Example B1 (not approved OPR item):**
> O&M staff must be given the opportunity to get an overview of the building's energy consumption on a monthly basis.

> **Example B2 (approved OPR item):**
> O&M staff must be able to create separate graphs of an optional month's electricity, water, heating and cooling consumption, separated for each floor, by means of a button on each display in the BMS system. Consumption must be displayed on the Y axis and 0.0 point must be 0. The time period must be displayed on the X axis and 0.0 point must be the start of the month.

When the OPR requirements are to be formulated with measurable parameters, they should be evaluated against which Cx Activities can be used to verify them. This can be, for example:

a. Review – the requirement is checked when reviewing the project material.

b. Test – the requirement is checked by testing.

c. Inspection – the requirement is visually checked during inspection.

5.6.3. Format and structure

All items in the OPR must contain the following information:

a. Unique ID number (e.g., 1, 2, 3) that does not change during the project.

b. Indication of who has set the requirement.

c. Specific reference to, definition or category of what the requirement covers (e.g. ”ventilation system”, "O&M”).

d. Description of the requirement. The formulation must contain measurable parameters and any references to applicable standards and safety requirements. If the requirement covers only a single specific installation, this must be specified.

e. Verification method and documentation (e.g., visual inspection, measurement, functional testing).

Additional information can be added that contributes to the overview and tracking:

f. Additional documentation (e.g., the stages at which the requirement must be verified).

g. Responsible person for follow-up (e.g., a specialist from the Cx Team).

It must be possible to lock the format of the OPR so that it is not possible to change the requirements after approval by the Owner.

The document should be tailored to each case and can be an Excel spreadsheet, Cx software www.CxPlanner.com or a Word document. It is recommended that the chosen format ensures valid traceable history and the possibility for all participants in the project to access it at any time.

The OPR must be treated as a stand-alone document so that all requirements can be viewed in their entirety.

Figure 8 shows how the OPR can be built up.

ID	Category	OPR description	Creator	Reason for item	Verification method	Verification documentation
112	BMS	It must be possible to access the BMS system from an arbitrary place via the internet so all PC's in the O&M organization can be used.	TTJ	To achieve flexibility, O&M staff must be able to access the BMS system from all locations.	Review / Test	Review report & Test report
113	BMS	The BMS must be designed with 25% extra capacity for each point type, AI, DI, AO, DO and bus, both physically and in software.	TTJ	To ensure that future expansions are possible.	Review / Visual check	Reported in the Cx Log

Figure 8. Example of the structure of an OPR document.

5.6.4. Preparation of the OPR

The OPR must be drawn up in cooperation with the Owner, the Owner's O&M staff and end users (for example, shop owners, students, etc.). It is the responsibility of the Cx Team to complete the process of preparing the OPR. There are several methods that the Cx Team can use to develop the OPR, such as Nominal Group Technique[10], workshops and meetings.

The methodology chosen by the Cx Team must ensure that all stakeholders are involved and project-critical areas are identified. The Cx Team must have examined the participant's specialist knowledge in advance in order to adapt the methodology to the individual users in the workshop.

There may be cases where participants do not have the technical knowledge to set measurable technical requirements. Here, the Cx Team must ensure that the participant's requirements are reshaped and elaborated with the necessary technical specifications.

Every effort should be made to ensure that all key persons are involved in the preparation of the OPR. The Owner's key personnel can often be divided into two groups: "Direct Users" and "Indirect Users". The direct users are the O&M staff and the end-user who actively uses the building. Indirect users can be, for example, energy and finance departments.

When preparing the OPR, the Cx Team should take into account that the

[10] Structured method for brainstorming in larger groups.

requirements are designed in such a way that the Owner can reuse them for other projects. This can be done by marking generic requirements so that the Owner can see which requirements can be used in other construction projects.

The Owner must approve all the requirements to be used in the Cx process.

See section 10.3, “The OPR document” for examples of OPR requirements.

5.6.5. Implementing the OPR into the project

The OPR is a stand-alone document to complement the project material. It must always be part of the project material, so that everyone involved is always informed about the requirements. Consideration should be given to whether the OPR should be included in the project material or whether the OPR should be attached as an annex.

There may be cases where the OPR can only be verified in the Occupancy and Operations Phase; for example, a refrigerator’s performance or indoor climate. In these cases, it should be examined whether the OPR items can be included in the contractual documents, specifying that the verification will first take place during the Occupancy and Operations Phase. If possible, a test paradigm should be developed and included as it will contain the necessary information for verifying the OPR items. The following information should be included and detailed:

a. Prerequisites of the Cx requirement.
b. Period of operation during which measurement/verification is carried out.
c. How the measurement/verification is carried out.
d. Who performs the measurement/verification.
e. When the measurement/verification is to be carried out.
f. Whether the measurement/verification is dependent on the Contractor having delivered O&M.
g. Specific prerequisites that must be met for the measurement/verification to be accurate and to be carried out.

5.6.6. Lack of the OPR

There may be cases where the Cx process has started too late and therefore the OPR has not been prepared. As a rule, a Cx process does not exist if there is no OPR. However, this does not mean that the project cannot benefit from the use of the various Cx Activities.

If the project material has already been prepared, for example the Construction Documents, it may form part of the basis of the OPR. Depending on the level of detail of the project material, it will be possible, to a greater or lesser extent, to extract the OPR items directly from the project material.

Often, the Contractor's own QA/control plans in the project material can be used to specify verification requirements, while the expected documentation delivery can provide the framework for the Systems Manual.

However, the Owner must be aware that the implementation of the OPR at this time may be a change to the Design Team or Contractor's agreement, which may entail a change in their payment (additional work) and/or extension of time.

5.6.7. Deviation/dispensation of an OPR item

There can be no deviation from the OPR without the Owner's written approval. The deviation from an OPR item may be caused for several reasons, but the Owner must still approve the deviation. In the event of a deviation, the reasons for the deviation, the expected consequences and the cost must be described. The reason for a deviation can include, for example:

a. Errors in design or execution that have made it too costly or impossible to correct the error.

b. The desired solution (the OPR item) increases the cost of the construction project.

c. Technological developments have provided new opportunities to solve/meet the OPR item, but the solution differs from the OPR.

A deviation from an OPR item can be divided into two categories:

1. **Dispensation** - which can be carried out before the OPR item is waived.
2. **Deviation** – if the OPR item has been waived before receiving approval

from the Owner.

5.6.8. Structure of a deviation/dispensation application

In the case of a dispensation/deviation application for an OPR item, all information about the individual item must be included. The application must enable the Owner to make the choice about the approval of the dispensation/deviation on an informed basis. As a minimum the following information must be included:

a. Reference to the OPR item.

b. Description of the OPR item.

c. Basis of Design for the OPR item.

d. The name and date of the applicant.

e. Reasons for the application.

f. The economic impact that the deviation may have.

g. Consequences of deviation from the OPR item.

h. The Cx Provider's recommendation in relation to the deviation.

See section 10.2, "OPR: Exemption application" for an example of a waiver application.

5.7. The Commissioning Plan

Requirements from	Perform activity	Prepare document
ASHRAE G0	**Required**	**Required**
ASHRAE STD 202	**Required**	**Required**
DS 3090	**Required**	**Required**

The Cx Plan describes which Cx Activities are to be carried out, when they are to be carried out and who is responsible for their implementation. The Cx Provider is responsible for the Cx Plan and will prepare the first version of the Cx Plan in the Pre-Design phase, describing in detail the Cx Activities to be carried out in that phase. However, the Cx Plan must contain an overall description of all the Cx Activities expected to be carried out during the project.

The plan will need to be continuously adapted to reflect the decisions and choices made during the project. The Cx Provider is responsible for the continuous update in each phase and the detailed update to be made at each phase shift.

The Cx Plan should be seen as the Cx Team's work description; it is in this document that all future tasks of the Cx Team are described. In addition to this purpose, the Cx Plan will also be used to inform the other parties in the project about the Cx Activities. The various parties involved in the construction must be able to use the Cx Plan to gain knowledge of the Cx Activities in the project.

5.7.1. Level of detail

The Cx Plan must be updated at the end of each phase, with a detailed description of the Cx Activities to be carried out in the next phase of the project. When the project is in the Pre-Design phase, the level of detail of the Construction Phase will be low, but even at this level the Cx Plan must include an indication of the future Cx Activities.

The Cx Plan must be continuously developed to contain detailed and comprehensive descriptions and the parties involved must be identified. By ensuring a sufficiently high level of detail, the Cx Plan can be used as a working and information document across project participants.

At the end of the Cx process, a Cx Report must be drawn up. The Cx Plan may be the template for this if its level of detail is sufficiently high.

5.7.2. The commissioning plan as contract document

If the level of detail is sufficiently high, the Cx Plan may be used as an annex to the contract document of the agreement with the Design Team and the Contractor. The descriptions of the participation of the Design Team and the Contractor in the Cx Activities must be detailed and clearly indicate the specific works and deliveries. In addition to being applicable to the specific case, the Owner will be able to reuse it as a basis for future projects.

5.7.3. Content of the commissioning plan

The Cx Plan must contain as a minimum:

a. Description of the project and scope of the Cx process.

b. The roles, responsibilities and frequency of meetings of the Cx Team.

c. Communication flow and distribution of the Cx documents.

d. Time schedule and description of test activities.

e. Description of verification procedures and tools.

f. Handling of documentation.

g. Training and involvement of operating staff.

See section 10.4, "Table of Contents of the Commissioning Plan" for an example of a table of contents.

5.7.4. Structure of the commissioning plan

The design of the Cx Plan must be adapted to each project. It can be built up over the individual project phases or at an overall level of activities. The Cx Provider should clarify with the Owner whether the plan's structure should be generic, so that the Owner can reuse the structure for future projects.

If the plan is built up over the individual phases, it will be easier to include as part of the contract material and it can be used for the final Cx Report.

The text in the Cx Plan can be, for example, prose text or in tabular form. The following examples show how the different methods can be used. The examples are based on the activity, "Cx Design Review":

5.7.4.1. Example: Prose text

The example below is an extract from a Cx Plan. The extract is part of the section on Cx Design Review.

```
  ...
The Design Review starts when the tender project is complete and has
undergone internal quality assurance with the Design Team. It is a
prerequisite that internal quality assurance of the material has been
carried out before a Cx Design Review is carried out.
The project material shall contain all the items described in the Cx
Plan for the phase concerned and the handle all of the OPR.
  ...
A full review of the project material shall be carried out based on the
OPR and the BoD. The review shall be completed and reported in Cx
Design Review reports. A minimum of 2 weeks must be set aside for the
Cx Team's review of the project material. The period may not be
allocated to traditional holidays (industrial holidays).
  ...
The Design Team shall respond to all review comments. The review will
not be considered complete until all review comments have been answered
and the responses have been approved by the Cx Team.
  ...
```

5.7.4.2. Example: Table form

The example below is an extract from Copenhagen Airports' Cx Plan. The extract is part of the section on Cx Design Review.

The project material must contain:
Overall test schedule that shows that the master schedule includes tests.
The Test overview is completed with all plants in the project and test dates are inserted.
Inspection plans specifying what, how and when to check cf. Copenhagen Airports' project-specific performance description.

The project material must contain:
There must be requirements for the Contractor regarding detailed time planning of test activities, cf. section on test schedule.
The projects fire strategy must include the fire matrix and be part of the project material.
Documentation requirements as set out in the Systems Manual must be incorporated and the project-specific documentation process manual updated.
Description of test requirements for the individual disciplines, including requirements for execution/participation in joint testing ("pre-test").
The Cx contract documents and associated appendices must be attached.
All preconditions for "Cx test" must be clearly stated.

Table 3. Requirements for the content of the project material.

Process Requirements:
It is a prerequisite that the Design Team has performed self-inspection and QA of the project material before Copenhagen Airports' review begins.
The design manager will provide the Cx Team with evidence of the Design Team's internal cross-disciplinary reviews.
The Design Team will provide the Cx Team with evidence of their internal review during the design phases.
The Design Team must have a minimum of 3 weeks set aside for Copenhagen Airports' review of the project material. The time allocated is exclusively for review by Copenhagen Airports and may not be reduced or allocated to traditional holidays.
The Design Team must ensure that there are no outstanding/unresolved review comments before a phase shift takes place (e.g. from Design Development to Construction Documents). The review will not be considered complete until all review comments have been handled. If the Design Team indicates that the review comment first is incorporated in the next design phase, it is the Design Team's responsibility to ensure that the review comment is updated with the solution in the next design phase.
The Design Team must reply to all Copenhagen Airports' review comments within 10 working days of the submission of the Cx Review Report.
The Design Team must attend specialist follow-up meetings with the Cx Team if there is disagreement about the resolution of review comments.

Table 4. Requirements for the review process.

5.8. The commissioning log

Requirements from	Perform activity	Prepare document
ASHRAE G0	**Required**	**Required**
ASHRAE STD 202	**Required**	**Required**
DS 3090	**Required**	**Required**

The Cx Log is the management tool used to document, monitor and pursue observations made in the Cx process. The document is used throughout all phases of the project and constitutes the Cx Team's primary communication and follow-up document.

The Cx Log will be established in the Pre-Design phase by the Cx Provider, who will be responsible for it throughout the project. All parties in the project must have access to the Cx Log and all participants in the Cx Team must be able to enter information into it. However, the log must be structured in such a way that it is not possible to delete/remove data in it without the approval of the Cx Provider.

5.8.1. Format

The items in the Cx Log must contain, as a minimum:

a. Unique ID number *(e.g. 1, 2, 3)*.

b. Date of creation.

c. Name of creator.

d. Description of the observation.

e. Responsible party for carrying out the next action (e.g. clarification, rectification, response, control).

f. Field where dialogue, comments and status can be documented.

The format must allow for a traceable history so that it is clear at all times who has made a change to a log item. It must also be possible to see all previous comments and who wrote them.

The Cx Log can be, for example, an Excel spreadsheet, Cx software www.CxPlanner.com or a Word document. The document must be treated as a stand-alone document, which means that all log items must be visible in their entirety.

When resolving a task or problem mentioned in the log, at least the following must be documented:

a. Date of solution.
b. The name of the person who solved it.
c. The name of the person who updates the Cx Log.
d. Description of the solution.
e. If it has required one or more OPR items to be amended, the impact on the requirement(s) must be described and reference must be made to the deviation/dispensation report.

The Cx Provider must continuously ensure that the items in the Cx Log are updated with the status and decisions from the project. This includes, among other things, that the log must be updated with input from construction meetings, Cx meetings and steering group meetings which have an impact on the items in the log. It is important that only information that is of direct relevance to the Cx Team is inserted, as the Cx Log is not to be used as a meeting record.

All participants in the Cx Team must contribute with information to the Cx Log within their respective disciplines and knowledge areas. The Cx Provider will have specified in the Cx Plan a meeting sequence and structure in which all items in the Cx Log are reviewed.

The Cx Provider may delegate responsibility for the update of the entire Cx Log or specific items to the different actors in the Cx Team. However, the Cx Provider is responsible for following up and documenting the items.

5.8.2. Example of setting up the Cx Log

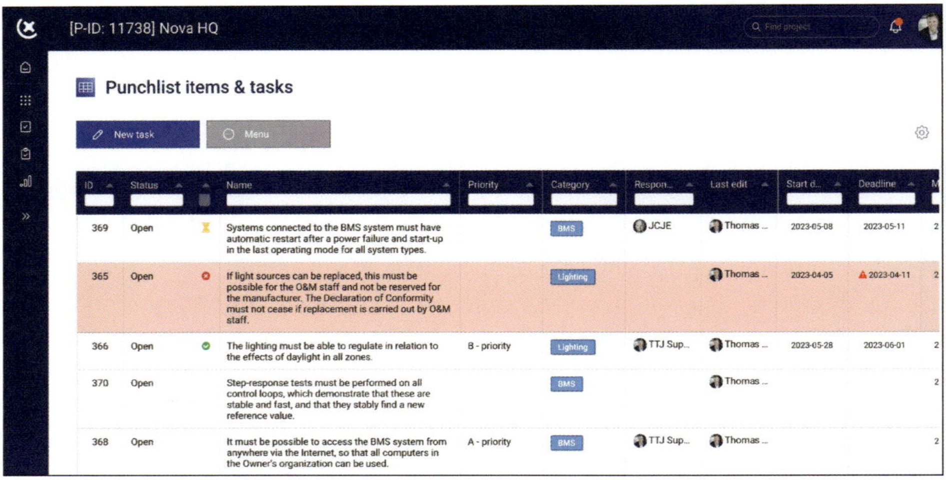

Figure 9. Example of setting up the Cx Log in CxPlanner.

5.8.3. An operational document

The Cx Log should be an integral part of all activities in which the Cx Team participates. The structure of the Cx Log must be flexible enough to include documentation from other Cx Activities such as the site inspections, discussion topics, review comments, test results, etc. In some cases, the Test overview may represent the Cx Log, see section 7.4, "Test overview" and section 8.5, "Managing the Test overview".

To ensure a valid and traceable history, and that all participants in the Cx organization can access the Cx Log, Copenhagen Airports use www.CxPlanner.com. One of the advantages of bringing all observations together in one place and using an online management tool is that all parties in the project can get an up-to-date overview of progress. Often the construction management uses it to gain an insight into outstanding works that may be obstacles to other activities, while several Contractor's use it to check that the interfaces to their disciplines are verified.

Figure 10 illustrates that all Cx observations and many of the Cx documents can be collected in the log.

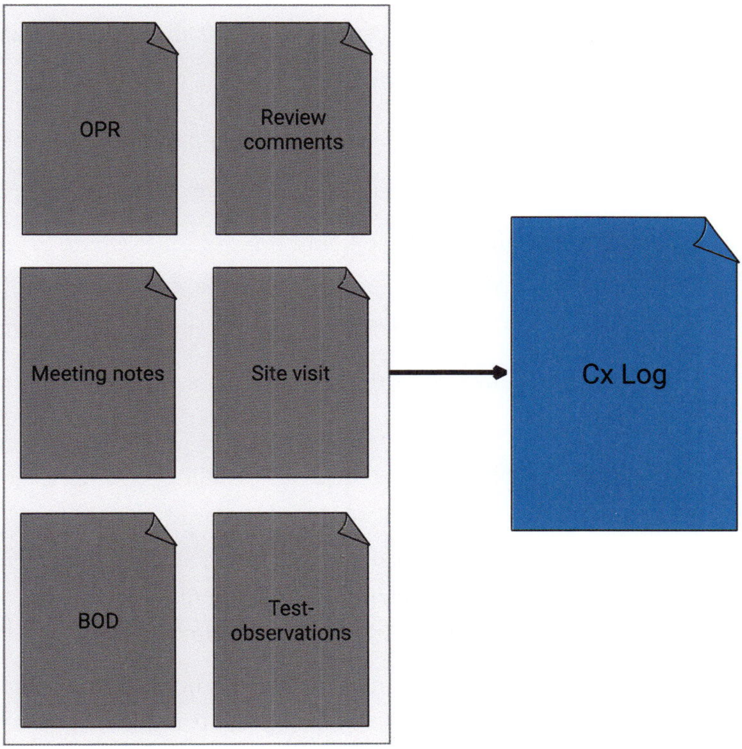

Figure 10. Many of the Cx documents can be collected in the Cx Log.

5.9. Cx Design Review

Requirements from	Perform activity	Prepare document
ASHRAE G0	**Required**	**Required**
ASHRAE STD 202	Not required	Not required
DS 3090	Not required	Not required

The Cx Team will carry out a multidisciplinary design review of the project material covering all installations described in the Cx Plan. The review will verify interfaces, operational capabilities and dependencies across installations and disciplines, with the primary purpose of ensuring compliance with the OPR.

Although the Cx Team reviews the project material, it is still the Design Team who is responsible for the content and quality at all times.

5.9.1. Coordination

The Cx Provider will manage and coordinate the Cx Design Review for the Cx Team. This requires access to the project material, as well as coordination of resources and structuring of the reporting. The review can be carried out in several different ways; for example, through workshops, meetings, individual reviews or multidisciplinary review meetings. The activities that the Cx Provider must manage are shown in Figure 11.

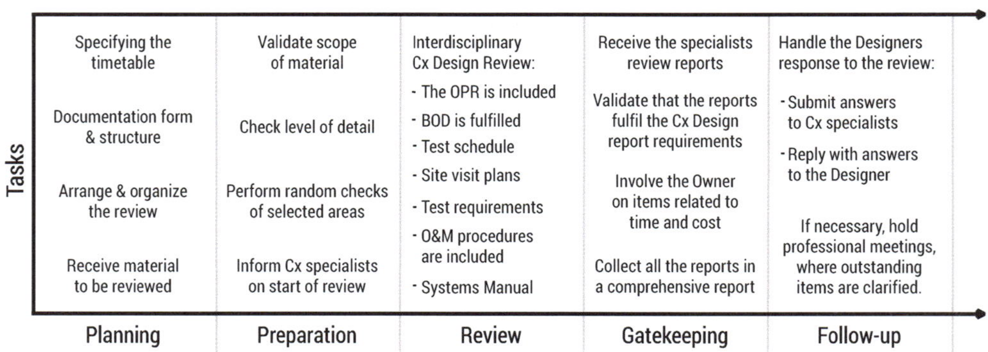

Figure 11. The Cx Provider's tasks during the review.

5.9.2. Scope of Cx Design Review

The scope of the Cx Team's review of the project material is scaled based on the size, complexity and finances of the project. If the Design Team has specific areas they wish to be reviewed, this must be disclosed to the Cx Provider. However, the Design Team still remains fully responsible for the content and quality of the project material at all times.

The scope of the review must be described in the Cx Plan and approved by the Owner. For example, the scope can be specified as one or more of the following:

a. All project descriptions for technical areas described in the Cx Plan are checked.

b. 100% control of all functional descriptions.

c. 10% of all specifications and in case of errors the scope is increased to 100%.

d. Drawings are divided into a grid, e.g. with fields corresponding to 5x3, where 3 fields corresponding to 20% are checked.

5.9.3. Prerequisites for the review

It is a prerequisite that the Design Team has performed self-inspection and quality assurance of the project material before the Cx Team's review begins. The Design Team will provide the Cx Provider with evidence of their internal quality assurance of the project material.

5.9.4. Introduction meeting

The Cx Provider must decide whether to hold an intro meeting where the Design Team presents the project material for the Cx Team. The purpose of an intro meeting is to provide the Cx Team with a quick insight into the structure and content of the project material, so that the subsequent review can be carried out efficiently. At an intro meeting, general questions, such as technical solutions, etc. could be clarified before the start of the review.

5.9.5. Performing the review

The Cx specialists carrying out the Cx Design Review must have the necessary skills to understand multi-disciplinary installations and systems. The primary purpose of the review is to verify that all the requirements in the OPR are met in the project material. In addition, it must be ensured that the solutions chosen are operational and energy efficient. Often, the Cx Design Review will be structured around these four elements:

a. General quality review of the project material, including readability and level of detail.

b. Coordination and interfaces between the different disciplines.

c. Options for verification of the selected solutions.

d. Compliance of the project material with the OPR (and with the BoD when it has been prepared).

5.9.6. Cx Review report

The review must be documented in a review report, where each review comment must contain:

a. Unique ID number *(e.g. 1, 2, 3)*.

b. Date of creation.

c. Name of creator.

d. Description of the review comment.

e. Responsible party for carrying out the next action.

f. Dialog, comment, and reply field.

When following up on the review comments, there must be traceable history in which it is possible to see previous comments and who wrote them.

The Cx Design Review report can be, for example, an Excel spreadsheet, Cx software www.CxPlanner.com or a Word document. There is no formal requirement for the format, but the review report should be treated as a stand-alone document. This means that all the review items must be visible in their entirety.

5.9.7. Review focus areas

The review will verify that all:

a. The items in the OPR are addressed and fulfilled in the project material.

b. Interfaces across contract boundaries and disciplines have been identified and described.

c. Solutions have been selected with a focus on the subsequent O&M.

d. Solutions consider energy efficiency and sustainability.

e. Verification and testing requirements are included.

5.9.8. Follow up on review comments

The Design Team will respond to all review comments from the Cx Team. The Design Team will also ensure that there are no outstanding/unresolved review comments before a phase shift takes place.

The review will not be considered complete until all review comments have been handled. If the Design Team indicates that a review comment can be incorporated or handled in the next design phase, it is the Design Team's responsibility to ensure that the review comment is updated with the solution in the next phase.

5.9.9. Example of review report

Figure 12 shows how a review report in the Cx software www.CxPlanner.com.In the example, the comment is specified in the column "Name" and the document to which the comment refers is specified in "Document".

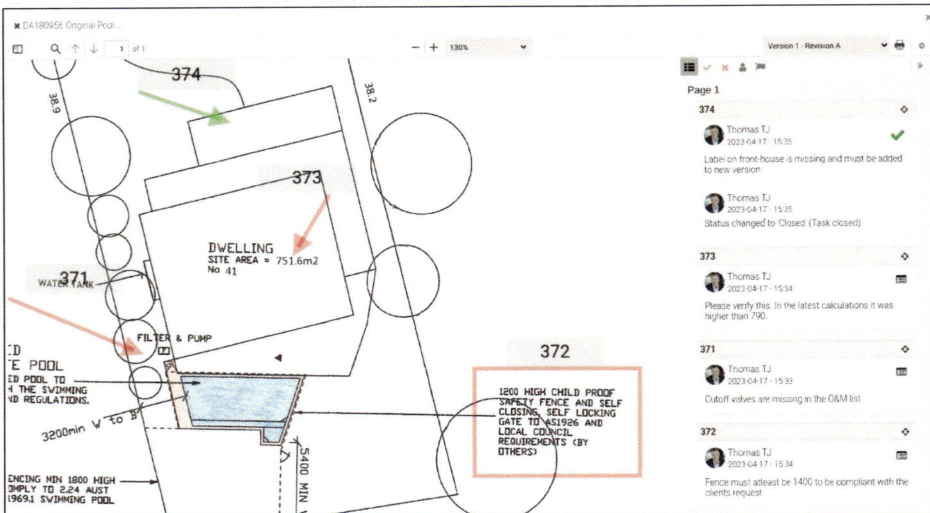

Figure 12. Example of review report.

Figure 13 shows how a review comment can be answered using Cx software www.CxPlanner.com. By using this type of digital solution, a valid and traceable history is ensured.

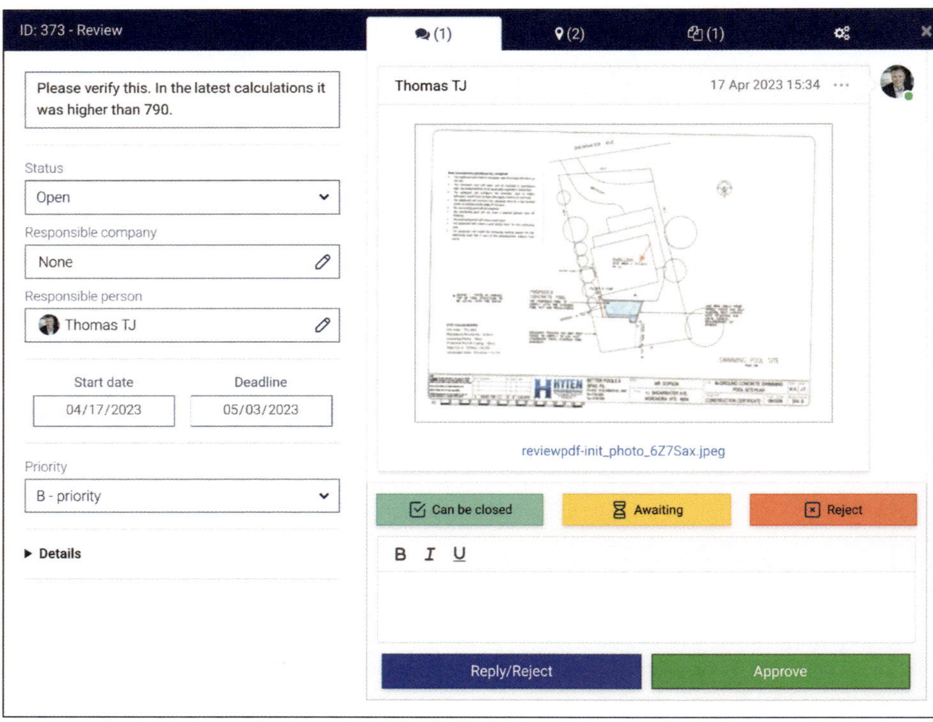

Figure 13. Example of response to review comment.

5.10. Phase acceptance

Requirements from	Perform activity	Prepare document
ASHRAE G0	**Required**	**Required**
ASHRAE STD 202	Not required	Not required
DS 3090	**Required**	**Required**

At the end of a project phase, the Owner must approve that the phase is completed and the Cx process will continue in the next phase. It is the Cx Provider who prepares the phase approval document and presents it to the Owner.

5.10.1. Contents

The phase approval document must contain:

a. Description of the items from the OPR which are deviated from.

b. Summary of the cooperation in the Cx Team.

c. Evaluation of the Cx Activities carried out.

d. Summary of open, closed and settled review comments.

e. The Cx Plan, the OPR and the Cx Log will be annexed to the phase approval document.

5.10.2. Format

The format of the acceptance document must be reconciled with the Owner when drawing up the Cx Plan. There are no official requirements for the format and structure of the document.

5.10.3. Acceptance from the Owner

The Owner must approve in writing that the Cx Process can continue. Acceptance can be made by e-mail or signature on the acceptance document.

5.10.4. Example of content in the acceptance document

The examples below show different acceptance documents. Table 5 shows how the acceptance document can be constructed in schematic form, while Figure 14 is showing an acceptance document written in a letter format.

Project Phase	Pre-Design
Cx Provider	Thomas T. Jarløv
Cx Team	Everyone who is part of the Cx Team is listed by name, company and their area of responsibility in the Cx Process. For example: - Participant 1, Company & Responsibility - Participant 2, Company & Responsibility
OPR	A summary of the work with the OPR must be made. Particular attention should be paid here to possible deviations and changes. - Deviations - Changes - Additions
Review	The review process and its results are summarized. Only the most important review comments, which may have an impact on time and economy, should be included. - Process - Comments - Outstanding
OPR	Work on the Cx Log is reviewed. - Critical items - Risks - Reduced risks
Evaluation	The Cx Providers assessment of the past phases and cooperation between the different parties. - The process - Cooperation with the Design Team
Phase Approval	Owner's approval, e.g. by signature.

Table 5. Acceptance document in schematic form.

If letter format is required, this must be approved by the Owner. In most cases, the letter format will have to be supplemented with Table 5 as an attachment.

Phase acceptance

Pre-Design

In the Pre-Design phase all Cx Activities according to the Cx Plan section 3.4 have been performed.

Documents related to these Cx Activities have been updated. This includes:
- OPR
- Cx Log
- Cx Plan

OPR item has identification number 102.

OPR item number 102 is waived with approval by the Owner. Deviation and relations to other OPR items is described in the exemption application TXXT_CR02. All review comments for the project material is clarified and completed. The review comments can be found in the Cx Design Review report TXXT_GB_001. The commissioning process is performed according to contractual agreement and may continue into the phase.

Sign, Owner

Sign, Cx Provider

Figure 14. Acceptance document in letter form.

6. Design Development

This section deals with the phases of the Design Development, which are spread over 2 phases. In some cases these phases will be joined into one.

a. Schematic Design

b. Design Development

FIDIC defines the "Schematic Design" and "Design Development" as:

Schematic Design

> The Schematic/Preliminary Design Phase generally involves the application of a design idea to the practical implementation of the desired capital project. It's is the phase where sufficient design concepts are developed for the client and (sometimes) regulatory authorities. This phase will permit the feasibility of a project, development potential of a site, or the selection of one particular conceptual approach over others for the client to pursue
>
> — FIDIC, Definition of Services Guidelines (Civil Works) 2016

Design Development

> This is the phase where the scope of all design components is clearly defined and coordinated. This may involve production of detailed information along with sketch details of all significant components and their interrelationships. This phase is where each technical expert prepares documentation to define the scope of all project elements. Major input is required from all designers on the team.
>
> — FIDIC, Definition of Services Guidelines (Civil Works) 2016

6.1. Commissioning activities

Activity	Document	Description
Hold a start-up meeting	Meeting agenda & minutes	Hold a start-up meeting with the Design Team where the Cx Activities are reviewed.
Prepare BoD	BoD	The Basis of Design document contains the Design Teams descriptions of how OPR items are expected to be met.
Documentation requirements	Systems Manual	Requirements for documentation formats, content and structure specified in the Systems Manual.
Cx Design Review	Review report	An interdisciplinary review is performed of the project material which is documented in review reports.
Update Cx documents	Cx documents	All Cx documents must updated, with decisions and details.
Phase acceptance	Acceptance document	The Owner must approve the performed Cx Activities and, that the Cx Process continues in the next project phase.

6.2. Start-up meeting with the Design Team

Requirements from	Perform activity	Prepare document
ASHRAE G0	Not required	Not required
ASHRAE STD 202	Not required	Not required
DS 3090	Not required	Not required

A start-up meeting with the Design Team must be organized where the Cx Activities for the next phases are reviewed. If a new Design Team is appointed during the phases, a new start-up meeting must be held.

The design phases include special Cx Activities that the Design Team may not have worked with before. The Cx Provider must therefore ensure that the Design Team has understood which works and deliveries they are responsible for.

The start-up meeting must, as a minimum, include:

a. General introduction to the Cx process

b. BoD – the purpose of the document and how to respond to each OPR item.

The meeting may be extended to include:

a. The Test Overview – format, structure, level of detail and how it can be combined with the project installation overview.

b. Test schedule - requirements for the structure and sequencing of tests.

The general requirements for the start-up meeting are described in section 5.5, "Start-up meeting with the Design Team".

6.3. Basis of Design (BoD)

Requirements from	Perform activity	Prepare document
DS 3090	**Required**	**Required**
ASHRAE G0	**Required**	**Required**
ASHRAE STD 202	**Required**	**Required**

The BoD is a separate document containing specifications and description of how the Design Team expects to fulfil the OPR. The Design Team must describe how they intend to resolve each individual OPR item. The description is an early verification and expectation alignment of the OPR item between the Design Team and the Cx Team.

The BoD must be a dialogue-based tool that the Design Team and Cx Team collaborate on.

The BoD systems and structures the Design Team's thoughts and plans, so that the Cx Team can verify at an early stage that the Design Team has adhered to the OPR. In addition to being a verification document for the Cx Team, the BoD is also a tool for the Design Team. Through the BoD, the Design Team can inform the Cx Provider and the Cx Team at an early stage of the design process that an OPR item cannot be fulfilled in the project. This will create a proactive approach to dealing with deviations.

The document must be prepared by the Cx Provider, while it will be completed by the Design Team before starting the design process itself. The Design Team will prepare a BoD-statement for each individual item in the OPR.

Figure 15 contains a BoD-response in the field on the right, while the OPR item is specified in the field on the left. The BoD-response in this case is an action which the Design Team will perform to ensure compliance with the OPR.

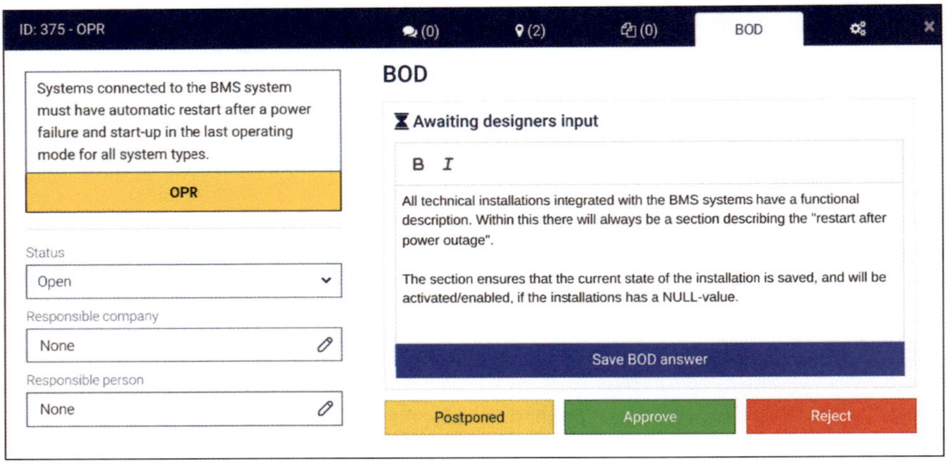

Figure 15. BoD-response to an OPR item in www.CxPlanner.com.

6.3.1. Developing the BoD

The BoD is not a standardized document in construction projects, and there are many Design Teams who have not worked with the BoD before. There may, therefore, be a risk that the Design Team's work with the BoD does not meet the Cx Team's expectations and therefore does not provide the necessary value for the Cx process.

The Cx Team must, therefore assist, and support the Design Team in making BoD responses. It is recommended that the Cx Team prepare the layout of the document and set up the structure, after which meetings are held where the Cx Team helps the Design Team to complete the document.

6.3.2. Structure of the BoD

The BoD should be constructed in the same format as the OPR, as this allows reuse of the structure from the OPR. This is an advantage, as the Design Team has to prepare a BoD for each individual OPR item. If the Cx Team has chosen to use the Cx Log as the master document (see section 5.8, "The commissioning log"), the BoD should be included in it to ensure a comprehensive overview.

The BoD must, as a minimum, include the following information:

a. Reference to the OPR item to be answered.

b. Description and explanation of how the requirement is expected to be resolved in the project.

c. The name of the responsible person from the Design Team for the BoD response.

d. Date of the BoD response.

6.3.3. Level of detail

The BoD response must be sufficiently detailed for the Cx Team to assess that the Design Team will satisfy the OPR item in the project. It can be challenging for the Design Team to describe a detailed solution early in the project, as at an early stage, for example in the Schematic Design phase, there are often many unresolved elements that may have an impact on the choice of solutions in the project.

If the Design Team does not think it is possible to prepare a BoD response due to unresolved elements, these elements must be listed and the BoD response postponed until later in the project design. The BoD response must, therefore, be updated later in the project when the elements have been clarified. No element must be allowed to remain open indefinitely.

6.3.4. Approval of BoD response

It is for the Cx Team to check and approve the Design Team's replies in the BoD. Each BoD response must be reviewed and either approved or rejected by the Cx Team. If a response is rejected, the Cx Team must describe why the BoD response is rejected, and the Design Team must review and update the BoD response.

6.3.5. Updating the BoD

The Design Team must update the BoD if items have been added to the OPR or changes have been made to the project that affect already selected solutions. At each change, the Cx Team must verify that the BoD-response complies with the OPR.

6.3.6. Examples of BoD responses

The examples below show how a BoD response can be performed. In Table 6 (Example 1) a specific reference to the drawing fulfils the OPR, while in Table 7 (Example 2), a more general response is made.

Example 1	
Reference to OPR item	ID: 101 – It must be possible to block both sides of filters, dirt collectors and pumps.
Replying	Thomas TJ
Date	2021-01-06
BoD	Shut-off valves are installed on both sides of filters, dirt collectors and pumps. See TX_K0-0_666.

Table 6. Example of BoD-response (example 1).

Example 2	
Reference to OPR item	ID: 102 – Leak detection will be installed on strategic locations (minimum per floor) in the distribution system of the installations.
Replying	Thomas TJ
Date	2021-01-06
BoD	Leak detection is enabled by installing energy and flow measurements on supply and return lines respectively for relevant pipe sections.

Table 7. Example of BoD-response (example 2).

6.4. Systems Manual

Requirements from	Perform activity	Prepare document
ASHRAE G0	**Required**	**Required**
ASHRAE STD 202	**Required**	**Required**
DS 3090	**Required**	**Required**

The Systems Manual must contain all the documentation necessary to operate and maintain a building. This includes O&M documents, manuals, test reports, training plans, etc.

The Systems Manual can be symbolized as a large folder where all the paper documentation is inserted and structured. However, due to technological developments, it is more often seen that Owners want a digital delivery, rather than paper.

The Systems Manual must, therefore, be seen more as the framework and requirements for the documentation to be submitted and structured in a way that supports the Owner's O&M organization's use of it. Often this will include the establishment of maintenance plans in the Owner's database maintenance system, while the documentation is submitted in a database documentation system.

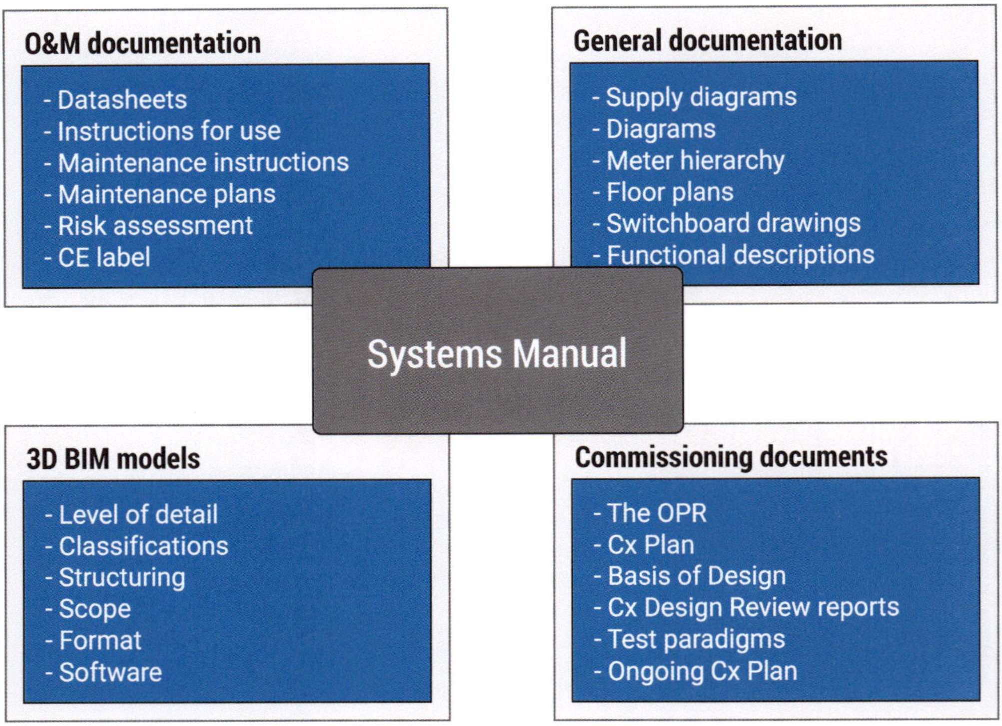

Figure 16. Illustration of the contents of the Systems Manual.

6.4.1. Documentation requirements

If the project uses a special documentation standard, this must form the framework for the Systems Manual. Often, most of the requirements for documentation will be reflected in the Owner's documentation standard, as it contains requirements for formats, delivery forms, etc. However, the Owner's documentation standard does not contain requirements for the Cx documents, so they must be described.

If a documentation standard is implemented on the project, it is important that the requirements from the Systems Manual are included. If the Owner has a database maintenance system, there must be requirements for the documentation to be submitted in formats that can be imported into it.

Specific requirements for the documentation can either be specified as OPR items or included in the documentation standard. For example, if there is no appendix describing O&M, this must be prepared.

6.4.2. File naming

It is important that requirements for file naming are set early in the project. If the Owner already has a file naming system, it must be used. Otherwise the Cx Provider can assist with specifying the requirements for it. However, the Cx Provider must ensure that there is a defined file naming system for Cx documents.

Figure 17 shows how the file naming structure can be set up. The file name must clearly indicate what material the file contains. A file naming manual must be drawn up that contains all the permitted values for the various parameters.

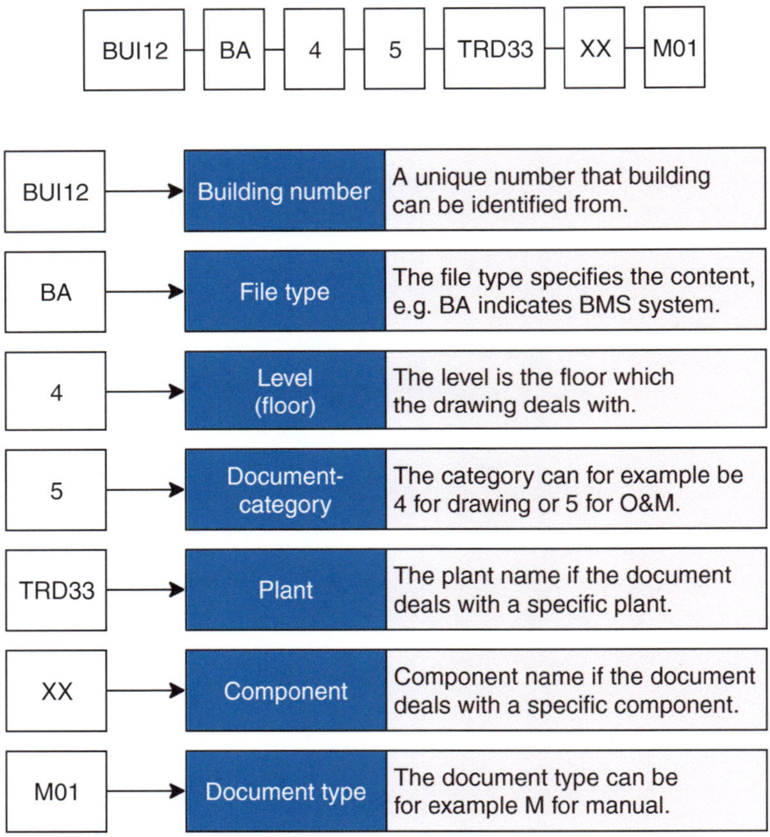

Figure 17. The structure of a file naming system.

6.4.3. Sample submission

Requirements for at least one sample submission of the documentation, and preferably more, should be included. The Cx Team, together with the project's documentation manager, must review the documentation submitted. The sample submission is an early check that the formats and structure comply with the requirements of the Systems Manual.

The sample submission should be at 30% and 80% during the Construction Phase, and must include at least one file from each subject area as well as an O&M plan for at least one system of each type. If tests or balancing have been carried out at the time of the sample submission, requirements must be made for these file types to be submitted as well.

6.4.4. Updating

The Systems Manual must be continuously updated by the Cx Team throughout the project process so that it always contains requirements for the current installations in the project.

6.5. Cx Design Review

Requirements from	Perform activity	Prepare document
ASHRAE G0	**Required**	**Required**
ASHRAE STD 202	**Required**	**Required**
DS 3090	**Required**	**Required**

Cx Design Review will verify by review and scrutinizing that the solutions chosen comply with the OPR. This includes, among other things, the review of calculations, CFD simulations, etc.

The review must follow the requirements set out in section 5.9, "Cx Design Review".

6.5.1. Content requirements

In addition to the fact that the OPR must be addressed in the project material, the project material must also contain:

a. Requirements for commissioning, handover and putting into service.

b. Requirements for O&M manuals.

c. The time schedule will include deadlines for commissioning and testing of technical installations.

d. Documentation requirements, including the Systems Manual (section 6.4, "Systems Manual").

e. Requirements for the Contractor regarding detailed time planning of test activities.

f. Fire strategy.

g. Description of test requirements for the individual disciplines.

h. The Contractor's participation in Cx.

6.6. Update Cx documents

Requirements from	Perform activity	Prepare document
DS 3090	**Required**	Not required
ASHRAE G0	**Required**	Not required
ASHRAE STD 202	**Required**	Not required

All Cx documents must be updated with the latest information if this has not been carried out during the project phase. The Cx documents must be prepared for the subsequent phase of the project.

6.6.1. The Commissioning Plan

The Cx Plan must be updated with observations and specifications from the completed phase. This must include, as a minimum:

a. Basis of Design (BoD)

b. Systems Manual

c. Cx Design Review

6.6.2. OPR

The OPR must be updated to the extent that the Owner has changed or added requirements.

6.6.3. The commissioning log

All observations to be followed up in the Cx process must be documented in the Cx Log. This must be carried out during the project phase in such a way that the Cx Log always contains the full overview and is updated.

6.6.4. Basis of Design (BoD)

If changes have been made to design solutions, the Cx Provider must ensure that the BoD is updated with them.

6.7. Phase acceptance

Requirements from	Perform activity	Prepare document
ASHRAE G0	**Required**	**Required**
ASHRAE STD 202	Not required	Not required
DS 3090	**Required**	**Required**

The Owner must approve in writing that the Cx Process can continue. All outstanding review comments must be attached to the acceptance document.

The requirements for the acceptance document are set out in section 5.10, “Phase acceptance”.

7. Construction Documents

During the Construction Documents phase, the detailed project material the Contractors will bid on must be drawn up. It is, therefore, important that the requirements for the Contractor's participation in the Cx process are clearly specified in it. All requirements for testing and commissioning must be described in the project material, so that the Contractor agrees with the Cx Activities.

The Cx Plan must be updated with detailed descriptions of the Cx Activities to be carried out in the Construction Phase and the first version of the Test overview and test schedule will be prepared.

FIDIC defines the "Construction Documents" as:

Construction Documents

> Detailed Design (Construction Documentation or Working Drawings) usually provides a level of documentation that clearly
> defines the design, specification and extent of all elements. The design should be comprehensively coordinated with all disciplines. The consultant's documentation should be considered 100% complete.
>
> — FIDIC, Definition of Services Guidelines (Civil Works) 2016

7.1. Commissioning activities

Activity	Document	Description
Hold a start-up meeting	Meeting agenda & minutes	Hold a start-up meeting with the Design Team where the Cx Activities are reviewed.
Site inspection	Site inspection plans	The Cx team must check that the site inspection plans verify the OPR items.
Develop the Test overview	Test overview	The Design Team must prepare the first version of the Test overview. In its current form, it constitutes a plant list.
Develop the test schedule	Test schedule	The Design Team must prepare the first version of the test schedule. In the Construction phase, the Contractor details it.
Requirements for the Contractor	Contract requirements	Kravene til entreprenørens deltagelse i Cx specificeres i projektmaterialet og kontrakter.
Cx Design Review	Review report	An interdisciplinary review of the project material, which is documented in a review report.

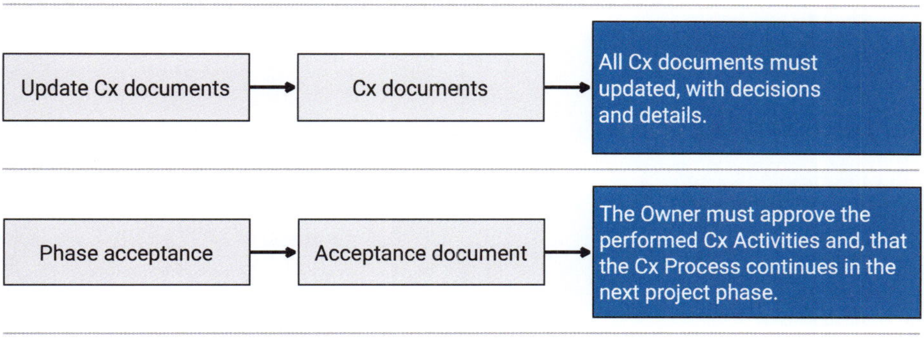
Update Cx documents
Cx documents
All Cx documents must updated, with decisions and details.
Phase acceptance
Acceptance document
The Owner must approve the performed Cx Activities and, that the Cx Process continues in the next project phase.

7.2. Start-up meeting with the Design Team

Requirements from	Perform activity	Prepare document
ASHRAE G0	Not required	Not required
ASHRAE STD 202	Not required	Not required
DS 3090	Not required	Not required

A start-up meeting with the Design Team must be organized where the Cx Activities for the next phases are reviewed. If the Design Team is the same as the one who participated in the previous phases and the Cx Activities for this phase have been reviewed, a start-up meeting is not necessary.

The start-up meeting must, as a minimum, include:

a. Site inspections - expectations of the site inspections plans and content.

b. The Test overview – format, structure, level of detail and how it can be combined with the project installation list.

c. Test schedule - requirements for the structure and sequencing of tests.

d. The Systems Manual - documentation requirements, sample delivery and delivery form.

The general requirements for the start-up meeting are described in section 5.5, “Start-up meeting with the Design Team”.

7.3. Site inspection

Requirements from	Perform activity	Prepare document
DS 3090	Not required	Not required
ASHRAE G0	Not required	Not required
ASHRAE STD 202	Not required	Not required

The Cx Team must be given the opportunity to influence and give input to the site inspection plans. In this context, care must be taken to ensure that the site inspection plans for the Design Team and Cx Teams do not overlap unnecessarily. Synergies need to be created between the two site inspections in order to establish the most effective process. A Design Team's site inspection manager, or a representative thereof, can usefully be connected to the Cx Team so that the site inspection manager is continuously informed about the Cx Team's observations and focus areas.

The site inspection plans and reports will be available to the Cx Team throughout the project.

The requirements for the Design Team's professionals performing site inspections may be described in the Cx Plan or the Cx requirements.

7.3.1. Requirements for the site inspection plans

There must be requirements for the Design Team to check and approve:

a. O&M documentation

b. Functional tests

c. TAB reports

d. Measuring reports

e. Test reports

The scope of the site inspection must be adapted to each project. If there are specific Cx requirements that the Design Team's site inspection can verify, the scope for that area should be set at 100%. As a general rule, the scope and level of detail of the site inspection plans will reflect the risk profile of the project.

In some cases, the Design Team's site inspections professionals only writes reports if they find any errors and deficiencies. The Cx Team must set requirements for site inspection reports to be created for critical installations at all times, even if there are no faults and deficiencies. These site inspection reports may form part of the final verification documentation.

7.3.2. First-time inspections

Site inspection plans must include First-time inspections when the assembly of major installations begins. The purpose of the First-time inspection is to detect any faults in the first of several identical installations. If a fault is found, it can be corrected on the next identical or similar installations before they are installed.

The Cx Team must assess the scope of First-time inspections of identical installations based on their complexity and criticality. The Design Team's site inspection professionals must notify the Cx Team before carrying out inspections at major installations. This will allow the Cx Team to participate.

Installations which should be included:

a. Automatic doors
b. Cooling system
c. Elevators
d. Emergency supply (diesel generator, UPS plant, etc.)
e. Escalators
f. Fancoils in IT-areas
g. Heating systems
h. Mechanical fire ventilation
i. Mechanical smoke venting
j. Ventilation systems

7.3.3. Specific focus areas

If the project includes critical installations, site inspection plans may be required to include 100% control of these. Specific focus areas may be, for example:

a. Energy meters (electricity, water, heating and cooling) used for balancing and testing and which the Cx Team and the Owner will use in the Ongoing Cx.

b. Fire alarm central for the overall control of the fire safety installations.

7.3.4. Continuous reporting

The Cx Team must use the Design Team's site inspection reports as supplementary verification documentation. The Design Team's site inspection must, therefore, be contractually obliged to inform the Cx Provider on an ongoing basis about the approval of O&M documentation, balancing, test, measurement and test reports.

7.4. Test overview

Requirements from	Perform activity	Prepare document
ASHRAE G0	Not required	Not required
ASHRAE STD 202	Not required	Not required
DS 3090	Not required	Not required

The Test overview is an extended list of plant, which keeps track of the individual plants' status and progress through the project. All plants' covered by Cx must be listed in the Test overview. Next to each plant, the individual verification activities must be visible, including functional test, balancing and Cx test.

The Test overview is not a document or tool described in *ASHRAE G0, ASHRAE STD 202* or *DS 3090*. However, it is a tool that helps in optimizing and structuring the tools in these standards. In some cases, the Test overview can even take over a large part of the tasks of the Cx Log.

7.4.1. Using the Test overview

As there are no requirements or guidelines for the use of the Test overview, this section is based on specific experiences from Copenhagen Airports. In 2015, Copenhagen Airports' Cx Team prepared and implemented the Test overview, and it has since been a management tool that has been used on all the Cx projects carried out.

One of the things that distinguishes the Test overview from the Cx Log is that it is built up over the individual plant items in the building. This means that you always have a concrete overview of each plant item, and that any challenges and obstacles are directly linked to it. By looking at it per item rather than per component, the Cx organization will have to relate to the item as a whole.

At Copenhagen Airports, the Test overview is included as a management and overview document for many of the parties in the projects. The project manager uses it to monitor technical progress and when the individual plant items are ready for commissioning. O&M personnel use it to monitor when it is time to perform inspections, while the Contractor's use it for test planning.

To create this common use of the Test overview, the Test overview must also be a central document in the project. This is achieved, among other things, by moving a large part of what the Cx Log would normally have contained to the Test overview.

The projects at Copenhagen Airports are of great diversity; therefore, the Test overview must always be adapted to the individual project. For larger projects with many BMS systems, for example, the Test overview will be expanded with a check that the BMS screens have been checked and approved.

7.4.2. Preparation of the Test overview

The Design Team must prepare the first version of the Test overview, which contains an overview of all plants included in the project. In this form, the Test overview will primarily constitute a plant list.

When the Test overview is handed in as part of the Construction Documents, the responsibility for the document is transferred to the Cx Provider. Thereafter, the Cx Provider will be responsible for updating and managing the information in the document.

7.4.3. Content requirements

The Test overview must contain the following fields:

Field	Description
Plant name	The name of the plant specified in the project.
Plant type/category	The category to which the system belongs, e.g. "Ventilation".
Location	Where the system is located, e.g. Room 105.
Machine manufacturer	The party responsible for the overall Declaration of Conformity.
BMS function description	Indicates that the final function description has been approved.
Balancing	Indicates that the balancing is approved. This can possibly be divided into several parts, e.g. "Balancing air" and "Balancing water".
Test	This is the Contractor's own test of the plant, cf. their QA plans and the tender control plans.
Pre-test	The Contractor's interdisciplinary tests have been performed (see section 8.12, "Pre-test").

Field	Description
Cx test	The final Cx test performed by the Cx Team (see section 8.15, "Commissioning test (SIT)").

Table 8. Requirements for content in the Test overview.

7.4.4. Scheduling tests

The Test overview can also serve as an overall test schedule. Next to each plant item, dates are given in their corresponding fields (for example for pre-test), which together with the outstanding fields gives a picture of when a test can be performed. The Cx Provider must assess whether the Test overview can constitute the test schedule (see section 7.5, "The test schedule").

7.4.5. Cx Progress Reports

As the Test overview must contain date indications, it can often be used by the Cx Provider for Cx Progress Reports on the technical progress and test activities (see section 8.4, "Commissioning Progress Reports"). By using visual indications for completed plants, for example by coloring them green, the Owner can quickly get an overview of how many plant items have been tested.

Often the project manager and construction management on projects will be able to benefit from the Test overview, as it gives them an insight into the completion of the technical installations. This knowledge can be combined with the prioritization of the Contractor's work tasks and focus areas.

7.4.6. Use of the Test overview throughout the project

Figure 18 shows an example of the use of the Test overview throughout the project. In blocks 1 and 2, data is collected in the Test overview, while the Test overview in block 3 is used for managing the tests, and in block 4 it is used for reporting.

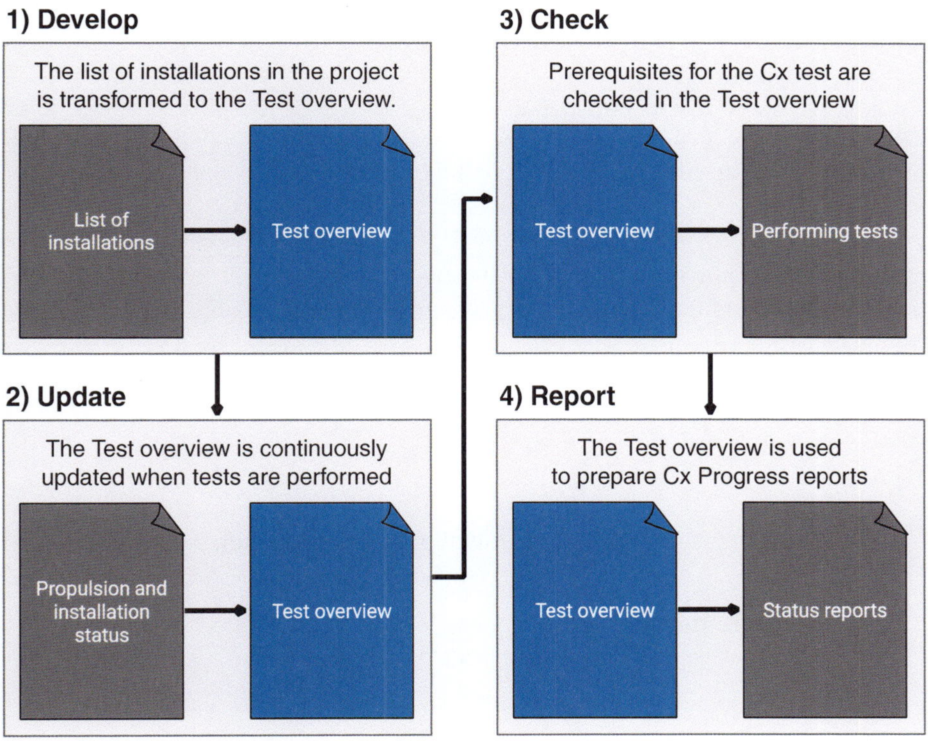

Figure 18. Use of the Test overview throughout the project.

7.4.7. Example

Figure 19 is an example of a Test overview from Copenhagen Airports built in the Cx software www.CxPlanner.com. The grey fields indicate that the item is not relevant for the plant. The green boxes are completed items, while the yellow ones are outstanding items.

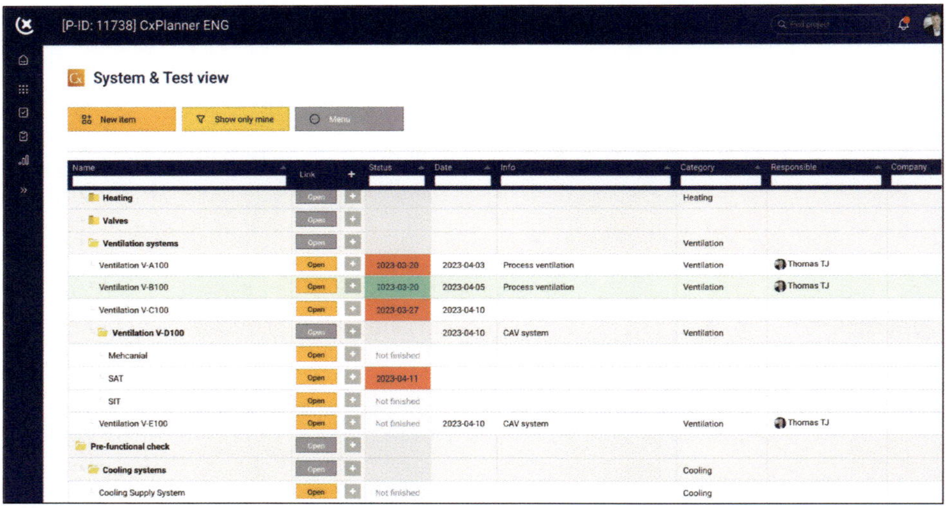

Figure 19. Example of a Test overview

7.5. The test schedule

Requirements from	Perform activity	Prepare document
ASHRAE G0	Not required	Not required
ASHRAE STD 202	Not required	Not required
DS 3090	Not required	Not required

The test schedule is a detailing of the main schedule, which only contains verification elements. The document must show that all installations are tested and balanced in the correct order and that sufficient time has been set aside for the various activities.

In the agreement documents, the Cx Provider may require that the Contractor's work-schedule has been carried out in sufficient detail, so that it can constitute the test schedule. The test schedule can, in some cases, consist of the Test overview (see section 7.4, "Test overview").

The test schedule for at least one of each system type (several systems working together) must show the coherence and in which order the different tests are to be performed.

7.5.1. Preparation of the test schedule

The Design Team must prepare an overall proposal for the test schedule, which shows that there is sufficient time to perform the test. The test schedule must clearly show the "Cx test period", which **only** contains Cx tests. Sufficient time must be set aside in the schedule for performing checks and tests, cf. the *Machinery Directive* and the Cx service description.

7.5.2. Format and content

The level of detail of the test schedule must be adapted to the project. For example, a detailed timetable block must be made for each type of system, after which it can be repeated as a template for other identical installations. This will force the Design Team to deal with the fact that sufficient time has been set aside for testing activities.

The form and structure of the document must ensure that it contributes to an efficient Cx process. If all tests are planned in detail in the software program MS Project, more time will often have to be spent updating the test schedule rather than the value that the test schedule should contribute. It can therefore be an advantage to use the method where detailed time is planned for one system per system-type.

It is important that the test schedule is a practical tool for those involved in the project. It must be possible for the Cx Team to use the test schedule, as well as the subcontractors on the project.

7.5.3. Test order

The test schedule must clearly show the order of interdependent tests. For example, it must be clear that the hydraulic systems have been pressure tested before balancing and that air volumes have been balanced before the BMS looptuning. Figure 20 shows an example of how the order can be built.

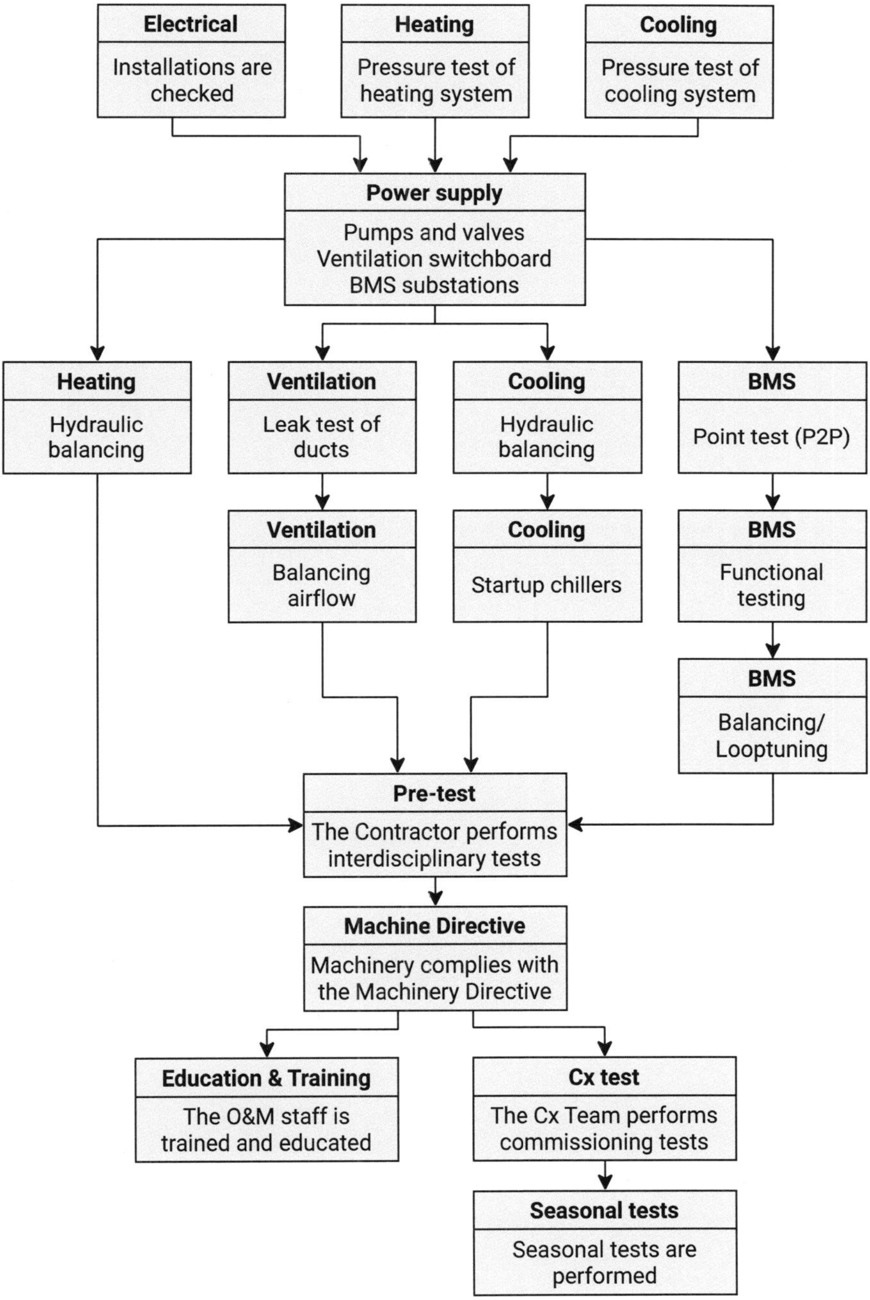

Figure 20. The illustration of the order of testing of different subject areas.

7.5.4. Example of a test schedule

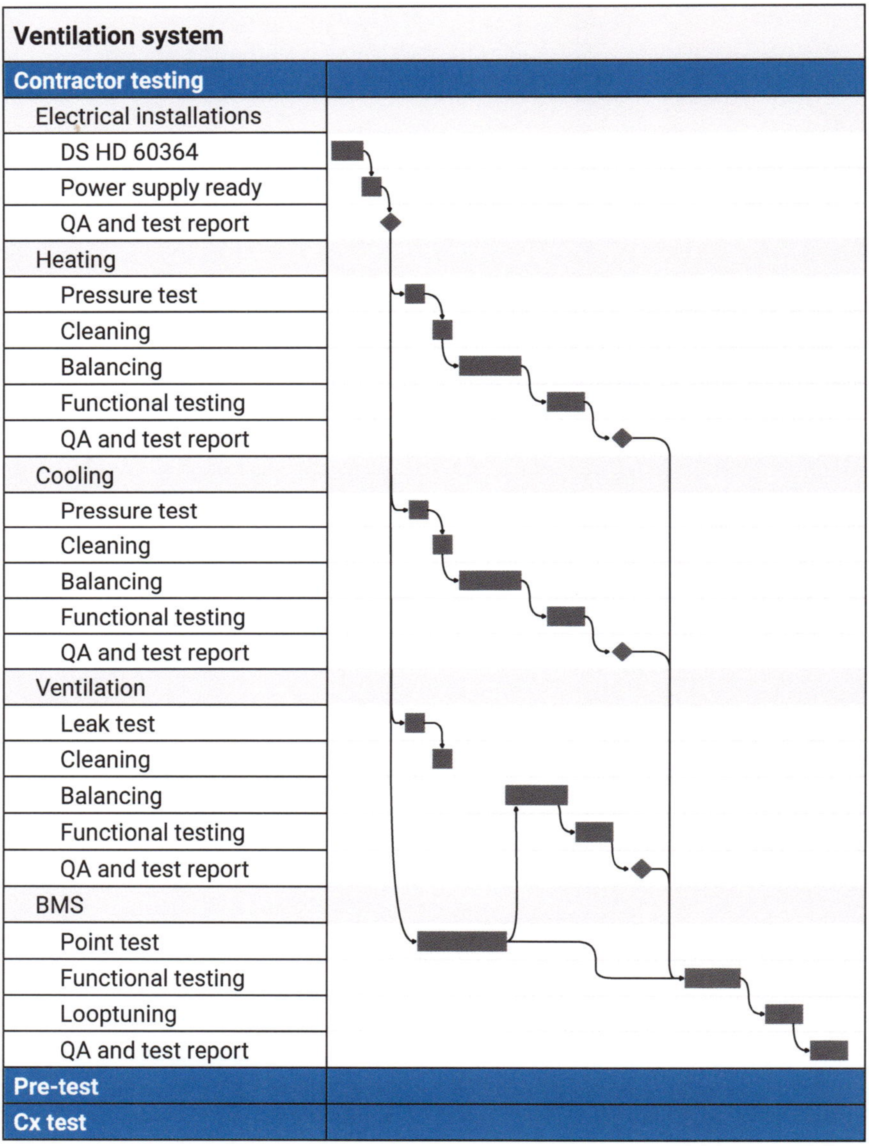

Figure 21. Example of a test schedule for a ventilation system which includes test activities for electricity, ventilation, heating, cooling, plumbing and BMS.

7.6. Requirements for the Contractor's participation

Requirements from	Perform activity	Prepare document
ASHRAE G0	**Required**	**Required**
ASHRAE STD 202	**Required**	**Required**
DS 3090	**Required**	**Required**

The requirements for the Contractor's participation in the Cx process must be clearly specified. The specific requirements for attending meetings, performing Cx Activities and preparing documents must be described in the project material and the Cx service description. This includes at least the entire section 8, *Construction Phase*.

7.6.1. QA, testing and balancing

The requirements for the Contractor's QA, balancing and testing must be described. For this, the test schedule (section 7.5, "The test schedule") is included as this shows the execution order of these. In addition, the prerequisites for the individual tests to be performed must be described.

7.6.2. Design made by the Contractor

If the Contractor needs to perform detailed designing of specific installations, the Contractor is required to follow the same rules and activities as the Design Team. It must be ensured that there is a requirement for a Cx Design Review of the project material.

7.7. Cx Design Review

Requirements from	Perform activity	Prepare document
ASHRAE G0	**Required**	**Required**
ASHRAE STD 202	**Required**	**Required**
DS 3090	**Required**	**Required**

The review must focus on the fact that it is possible to test and maintain the installations, so that their performance and functionality fulfil the OPR. The review must have an interdisciplinary focus, which means that functions across disciplines and boundaries must be checked.

Checklists must be prepared, which include the installations included in the Cx process. The checklists must help to ensure that the extent and known types of errors are checked.

The review must follow the requirements set out in section 5.9, "Cx Design Review".

7.7.1. Requirements for the content of the project material

In addition to the fact that the OPR must be addressed in the project material, the project material must also contain:

a. Requirements for O&M manuals.

b. Site inspection plans indicating how, when and what is controlled (section 7.3, "Site inspection").

c. A complete and updated Test overview (section 7.4, "Test overview").

d. Overall test schedule showing that the main schedule includes tests in the correct order (section 7.5, "The test schedule").

e. Documentation requirements, including the Systems Manual (section 6.4, "Systems Manual").

f. Requirements for the Contractor regarding detailed time planning of test activities.

g. The fire strategy.

h. Meter hierarchy (meter strategy).

i. Description of test requirements for the individual disciplines.

j. The Contractor's participation in the Cx process.

7.7.2. Sustainability

A sustainability review should be conducted, which focuses on energy optimizations, minimizing CO_2 emissions, cradle-to-cradle, demolition procedure, renewable energy and optimization of usage patterns. If the project is to be sustainability certified, the review should include the specific requirements of this sustainability certificate.

7.8. Update Cx documents

Requirements from	Perform activity	Prepare document
ASHRAE G0	**Required**	Not required
ASHRAE STD 202	**Required**	Not required
DS 3090	**Required**	Not required

All Cx documents must be updated with the latest information if this has not been carried out during the project phase. The Cx documents must be prepared for the subsequent phase of the project.

7.8.1. The Commissioning Plan

At the end of a design phase, the Cx Provider must update the Cx Plan with descriptions of the upcoming Cx Activities.

The update must, among other things, contain a description of the observations from the completed phase, so that the Cx Plan contains a detailed overview of the Cx Activities that have been carried out. The Cx Activities in the design phase must be described in detail, so that when the next phase begins, everyone knows their responsibilities and what deliveries are expected of them.

The update must, as a minimum, include:

a. Basis of Design (BoD)

b. Site inspection

c. Test overview

d. Test schedule

e. Systems Manual

f. Cx Design Review

At the end of the last design phase before the Construction Phase, the Cx Plan must be updated with a detailed description of the upcoming Cx Activities for the Contractor. The update must, as a minimum, include:

a. Test schedule and the integration with the project schedule.

b. The scope of test prerequisites and test activities.

c. Design to be made by the Contractor and Cx Design Review of this.

d. Systems manual and the documentation process.

e. Education and training of O&M staff.

f. Handover requirements.

7.8.2. OPR

The OPR must be updated to the extent that the Owner has changed or added new requirements.

7.8.3. The commissioning log

All observations to be followed up in the Cx process must be documented in the Cx Log. This is to be carried out during the project phase in such a way that the Cx Log always contains the full overview and is updated.

7.8.4. Basis of Design (BoD)

If changes have been made to design solutions, the Cx Provider must ensure that the BoD is updated with them.

7.9. Phase acceptance

Requirements from	Perform activity	Prepare document
ASHRAE G0	**Required**	**Required**
ASHRAE STD 202	Not required	Not required
DS 3090	**Required**	**Required**

The Owner must approve in writing that the Cx process can continue. All outstanding review comments must be attached to the acceptance document.

The requirements for the acceptance document are set out in section 5.10, "Phase acceptance".

8. Construction Phase

During the Construction Phase, installations and systems will be installed, tested, verified and put into service according to the OPR. The Contractor and subcontractors will become part of the Cx organization and participate in the Cx Activities.

Detailed planning of the tests to be carried out must be undertaken in the Construction Phase. The Cx Provider must manage and update the content of the Test overview continuously. The Owner's O&M staff must be trained in the use of the installations so that they can operate them from day 1.

During the Construction Phase, the work of the Cx Team will be intensified as more and more installations are installed. Specific Cx Site Inspections will be carried out to verify that the installed installations comply with the OPR. Cx Progress Reports must be provided to the Owner on an ongoing basis regarding the progress of the project.

At the end of the Construction Phase, multidisciplinary Cx tests must be carried out to verify that all the systems work according with the OPR and the Contractor must submit documentation in accordance with the Systems Manual.

8.1. Commissioning activities

Activity	Document	Description
Hold a start-up meeting	Meeting agenda & minutes	Hold a start-up meeting with the Contractor where the Cx Activities are reviewed.
Design by Contractor	Review reports	An interdisciplinary review of the project material, which is documented in a review report.
Progress reporting	Cx progress reports	The ongoing progress in the Cx Process is documented in Cx Progress Reports.
Managing the Test overview	Test overview	The Test overview is updated continuously during the phase with the status of the installations.
Planning of tests	Test schedule	A detailed planning of all test activities is performed with all the project participants.
Cx meetings	Meeting agenda & minutes	Regular Cx meetings, where the Cx log, the Test overview and Cx observations are reviewed.

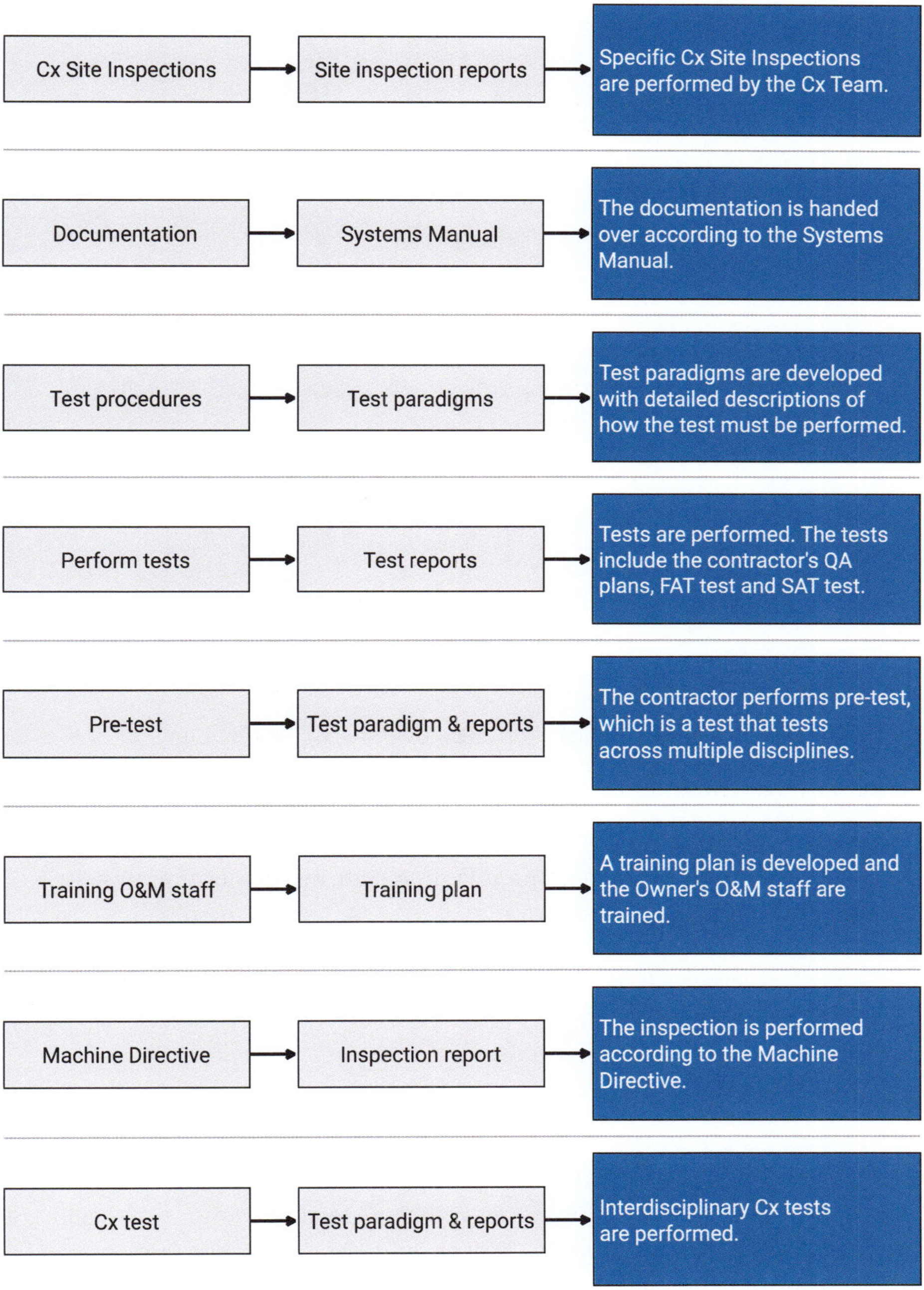
Cx Site Inspections
Site inspection reports
Specific Cx Site Inspections are performed by the Cx Team.
Documentation
Systems Manual
The documentation is handed over according to the Systems Manual.
Test procedures
Test paradigms
Test paradigms are developed with detailed descriptions of how the test must be performed.
Perform tests
Test reports
Tests are performed. The tests include the contractor's QA plans, FAT test and SAT test.
Pre-test
Test paradigm & reports
The contractor performs pre-test, which is a test that tests across multiple disciplines.
Training O&M staff
Training plan
A training plan is developed and the Owner's O&M staff are trained.
Machine Directive
Inspection report
The inspection is performed according to the Machine Directive.
Cx test
Test paradigm & reports
Interdisciplinary Cx tests are performed.

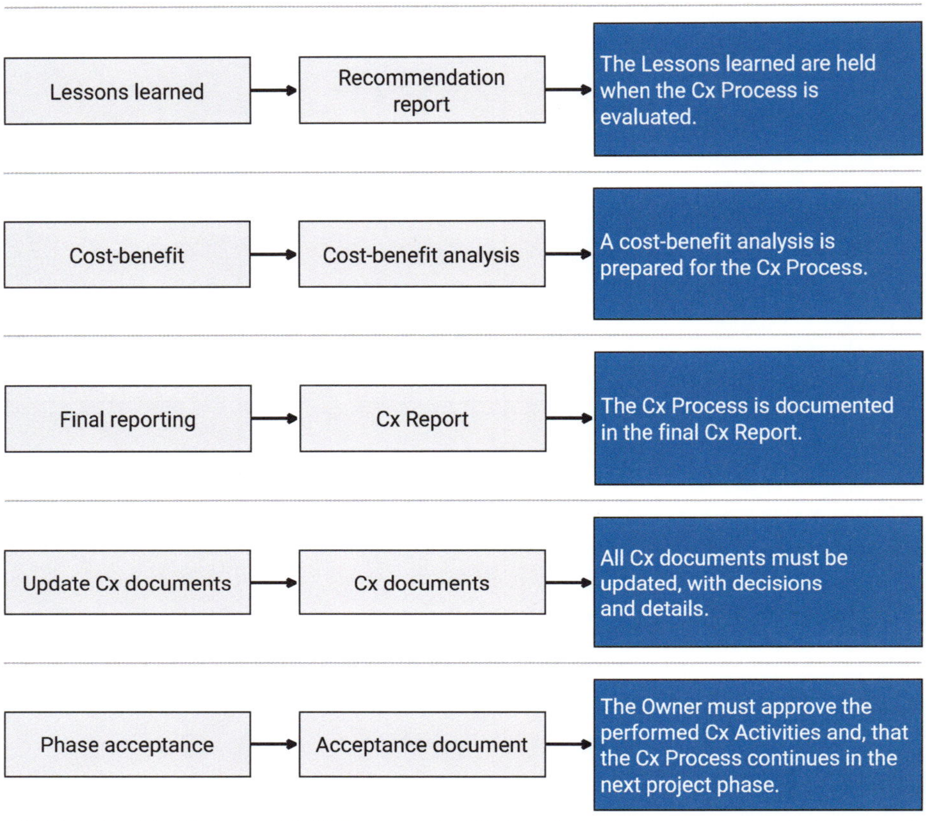
Lessons learned
Recommendation report
The Lessons learned are held when the Cx Process is evaluated.
Cost-benefit
Cost-benefit analysis
A cost-benefit analysis is prepared for the Cx Process.
Final reporting
Cx Report
The Cx Process is documented in the final Cx Report.
Update Cx documents
Cx documents
All Cx documents must be updated, with decisions and details.
Phase acceptance
Acceptance document
The Owner must approve the performed Cx Activities and, that the Cx Process continues in the next project phase.

8.2. Start-up meeting with the Contractor

Requirements from	Perform activity	Prepare document
ASHRAE G0	**Required**	Not required
ASHRAE STD 202	Not required	Not required
DS 3090	Not required	Not required

A start-up meeting, where the activities for the Construction Phase are reviewed, must be organized with the Contractor. The Construction Phase may include Cx Activities that the Contractor has not tried to work with before, such as the Test overview. The Cx Provider must, therefore, ensure that the Contractor has understood which works and deliveries they are responsible for.

The start-up meeting must, as a minimum, include:

a. Test overview – expected input from the Contractor and how the Test overview is used for continuous status overview.

b. Test schedule - review the level of detail.

c. Training and education - how to train the O&M staff.

d. The Machine Directive - expectation alignment of the manual, Declaration of Conformity and risk assessment.

e. Test – requirements for the Contractor's own tests, pre-tests and participation in Cx tests.

The general requirements for the start-up meeting are described in section 5.5, "Start-up meeting with the Design Team".

8.2.1. Involvement of subcontractors

If subcontractors, if any, do not participate in the start-up meeting, the Cx Provider must offer to hold a follow-up meeting where they participate. Subcontractors must participate in several of the Cx Activities; they must, therefore, understand their expected participation and be informed of any changes expected in their normal verification activities.

8.3. Design made by the Contractor

Requirements from	Perform activity	Prepare document
DS 3090	**Required**	**Required**
ASHRAE G0	Not required	Not required
ASHRAE STD 202	Not required	Not required

There may be cases where there is a requirement or custom for the Contractor to develop the final construction documents for certain parts of the project. This is often the case in the ventilation and sprinkling profession, for example.

When the Contractor is developing construction documents, it must be ensured that the project material complies with the OPR. The Contractor's project design must follow the same design requirements as the Design Team, and there must be requirements for a Cx Design Review to be carried out that follows the requirements specified in section 5.9, "Cx Design Review" and is documented in review reports.

8.4. Commissioning Progress Reports

Requirements from	Perform activity	Prepare document
ASHRAE G0	**Required**	**Required**
ASHRAE STD 202	**Required**	**Required**
DS 3090	Not required	Not required

The Cx Provider must continuously prepare Cx Progress Reports that provide an overview of the progress of the Cx Activities. The progress reports are an overview for the Owner of whether the project follows the planned timetable for the Cx Activities, whether there are delays and when Cx-related activities are completed.

The Cx Progress Reports may be used as additional documentation for phase approvals, where they are attached to the acceptance document. This will give the Owner an overview of the work carried out by the Cx Team during the relevant phase.

They can also be used if the Owner desires reports on the costs used by Cx Teams. Using an hourly summary schedule (see section 5.3, "Cost overview"), Cx Progress Reports can support what the Cx Team has achieved.

8.4.1. Contents

The following topics must be included in the Cx progress report if there are current changes since the last progress report.

a. Identified non-compliant installations and systems. The Owner must be able to form an overview of what impact it has on the project. A deviation from the OPR cannot be approved via the progress report, that must follow section 5.6.7, "Deviation/dispensation of an OPR item".

b. Carried out and completed Cx Activities since the last Cx progress report.

c. Description of changes to the timetable that have an impact on Cx Activities. Changes can be either delays or premature completion of work.

d. Tests performed and test results must be described. Once a system has been tested, the outcome of the test must be indicated in the Cx progress report. For this, the Cx Provider may consider using the Test overview (see section 8.5, “Managing the Test overview”), which provides a full overview of the systems and associated tests.

e. Summary of items from the Cx Log. This includes new items and how closed items were resolved.

f. Overview of expected Cx Activities before the next Cx progress report.

8.4.2. Scope

The scope and frequency of the Cx Progress Reports must reflect the size and complexity of the project. In the case of small projects of short duration, the Cx Provider will assess the value of producing specific Cx Progress Reports.

Often, samples of the various Cx documents could constitute the Cx progress report. For example, the Test overview can be used as a Cx progress report, as it contains a detailed overview of the technical completion of each installation.

8.4.3. Examples of commissioning progress reports

Progress reports can be performed in several ways; in section 8.4.4 a common table format is used, while in section 8.4.4.1 the Cx software www.CxPlanner.com is used.

8.4.4. Progress report example 1

Date	2010/week 5
OPR	**OPR item 314:** The wiring for the fan in the parking basement does not contain enough conductors to achieve a true feedback to the BMS system. According to OPR item 314 all installations must have a true feedback to the BMS system. The Design Team is investigating whether the true feedback can be obtained by a power supply relay. The problem here is that all fans are supplied from the same group in switchboard LS723. If this is not possible, the Contractor will request a deviation from OPR item 314. The Cx Team recommends as a starting point that the Owner does not accept this deviation, as the fans have a direct impact on personal safety in the parking basement due to NOX and CO.
Schedule	The schedule hasn't changed since Cx progress report 2021/week 4; all Cx Activities are still running at scheduled times.
Installations	The planned testing process is proceeding according to plan. Faults found during the tests are continuously rectified so that the installations can finally be transferred to the Owner's operation. As shown in the attached Test overview, 2 tests failed at week 5. These are the fans in the parking basement (see above section on OPR item 314) and electric heat tracing on the south side of the building. Electrical heat tracing failed as the power supply relay could not detect the low load. In the coming week, the cooling unit will be tested. This is a critical test for starting up the IT rooms, all of which require stable cooling. Pre-test has been performed with good results; therefore, it is expected that the Cx test will pass.
Cx Log	**OPR item 433:** During Cx Site Inspection of energy meters, it was observed that the red wire on the cooling energy meters (there are 1 red and 1 blue) was mounted on the return pipe. This is the opposite of the heat energy meter, where the red one is set on the supply pipe. The Cx Team has been in dialogue with the supplier, who has subsequently clarified that the red wire must always be mounted on the supply pipe. The Contractor has rectified this. The item is "Closed".

Upcoming Cx	**Pre-test** The Contractor's pre-test is ongoing and is expected to be completed within 2 weeks. **Cx Test** Cx testing is also ongoing and is expected to be completed within 4 weeks. **Season test:** During week 6, the functions and regulation of the cooling unit will be tested. However, due to the cold weather conditions, it will not be possible to carry out a capacity test. As a result, COP, step regulation and maximum performance will not be tested. These tests are planned to be performed at week 20.

Table 9. Example of a Cx Progress Report.

8.4.4.1. Progress report example 2

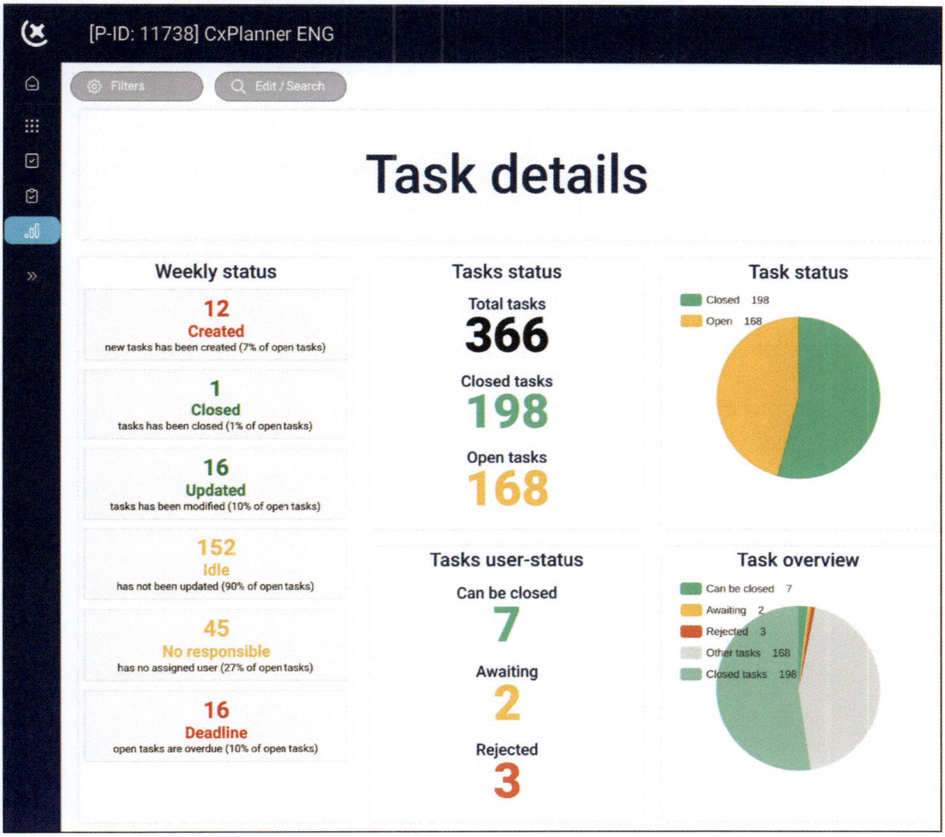

Figure 22. Progress report with www.CxPlanner.com

8.5. Managing the Test overview

Requirements from	Perform activity	Prepare document
ASHRAE G0	Not required	Not required
ASHRAE STD 202	Not required	Not required
DS 3090	Not required	Not required

The Cx Provider is responsible for updating and managing the Test overview, but the Contractor is required to continuously inform the Cx Provider about updates to be documented in it.

The general requirements for the Test overview are set out in section 7.4, "Test overview".

8.5.1. Follow-up

The Contractor is required to contribute information to the Test overview. When QA, balancing and tests have been carried out, the Contractor must inform the Cx Provider accordingly. The Contractor must maintain their own information and data in the Test overview.

The Cx Provider must continuously update the Test overview to provide at all times a true and correct view of all installations of the project.

a. The addition and/or removal of installations to the project must be reflected in the list.

b. Tests carried out, status, etc. must be stated.

If an online software solution is used to manage the Test overview, the Cx Provider may delegate responsibility to the Contractor to update their own data in the Test overview.

8.5.2. Coordination

During the Construction Phase, a series of meetings must be started, where the content of the Test overview is reviewed. At the meetings, the Test overview must be reviewed slavishly and the interfaces and prerequisites for the individual tests clarified.

Subcontractors who have detailed knowledge of their installations must participate, as it is often they who have an overview of the progress and any outstanding elements that can block future tests.

At the latest, 1 month before the start of the test period, weekly meetings of a duration of 1-2 hours are expected with, as a minimum, the participation of the Cx-responsible Contractor, BMS contractor and the Cx Provider. Consideration should be given to whether the project manager should also attend these meetings or may simply be on call. The meetings can usefully be started earlier so that any obstacles to testing are detected earlier. Often, these meetings can be combined with the periodic Cx meetings (section 8.7, "Commissioning meetings").

8.6. Test planning

Requirements from	Perform activity	Prepare document
ASHRAE G0	Not required	Not required
ASHRAE STD 202	Not required	Not required
DS 3090	Not required	Not required

The test schedule must demonstrate that the Contractor's quality assurance and tests of the various installations are placed in the correct order and show that sufficient time has been set aside for the individual test activities.

In some cases, the Test overview can be used for detailed test planning (see section 8.5, "Managing the Test overview").

8.6.1. Completion of the test schedule

The draft test schedule has been prepared by the Designer in the previous phase and attached to the tender documentation (section 7.5, "The test schedule"). The Contractor must adapt this to fit the Contractor's work-schedule.

8.6.2. Level of detail

The Contractor must schedule all testing activities for at least one system of each type in detail. The level of detail of the test schedule must be adapted to the project; for example, a detailed timetable block must be drawn up for each type of system, after which it can be repeated as a template for identical installations.

The test schedule must, as a minimum, include:

a. Testing, Adjusting and Balancing

b. Functional test

c. Checks for compliance with the *Machinery Directive*

d. Pre-test

e. Cx Test

8.7. Commissioning meetings

Requirements from	Perform activity	Prepare document
DS 3090	Not required	Not required
ASHRAE G0	**Required**	**Required**
ASHRAE STD 202	Not required	Not required

The Cx meetings will ensure that everyone involved in the Cx process is informed of progress throughout the Construction Phase and that there is always clarity as to who is responsible for performing the Cx Activities. The Cx meetings will deal with the technical aspects of the construction in relation to the Cx process. At the meetings, the Cx Log, Test overview and Test schedule must be reviewed.

Participants in meetings must have the necessary professional competence to deal with the matters they represent. In order to ensure effective Cx meetings, participants must also be decision-makers in their specific fields.

There should be no discussion of finances at meetings or the allocation of responsibility for errors. Meetings must have a practical, solution-oriented approach, with the common focus of complying with the OPR and ensuring momentum.

8.7.1. Coordination

The Cx Provider is responsible for convening, organizing and documenting all Cx meetings to be held throughout the Construction Phase. The topics will need to be continuously adapted to the state of the project, and people with the right professional skills will need to be involved, as necessary.

The Cx Provider will define the expected meeting series early in the project process, in cooperation with the Contractor.

8.7.2. Meeting summons

Notices of Cx meetings must include an agenda consisting, as a minimum, of:

a. Meeting Number
b. Time (start and end time)
c. Location
d. Attendee list
e. Issues to be discussed including:
    i. Outstanding actions from previous meetings
    ii. Upcoming Cx Activities
    iii. Focus areas from the Owner
    iv. Progress of the project compared to the timetable.

8.7.3. Meeting Minutes

The Cx Provider must draw up minutes of meetings and circulate them as soon as possible. The minutes should be circulated no later than 3 working days after the meeting unless otherwise specifically agreed with the Owner and the Cx Team.

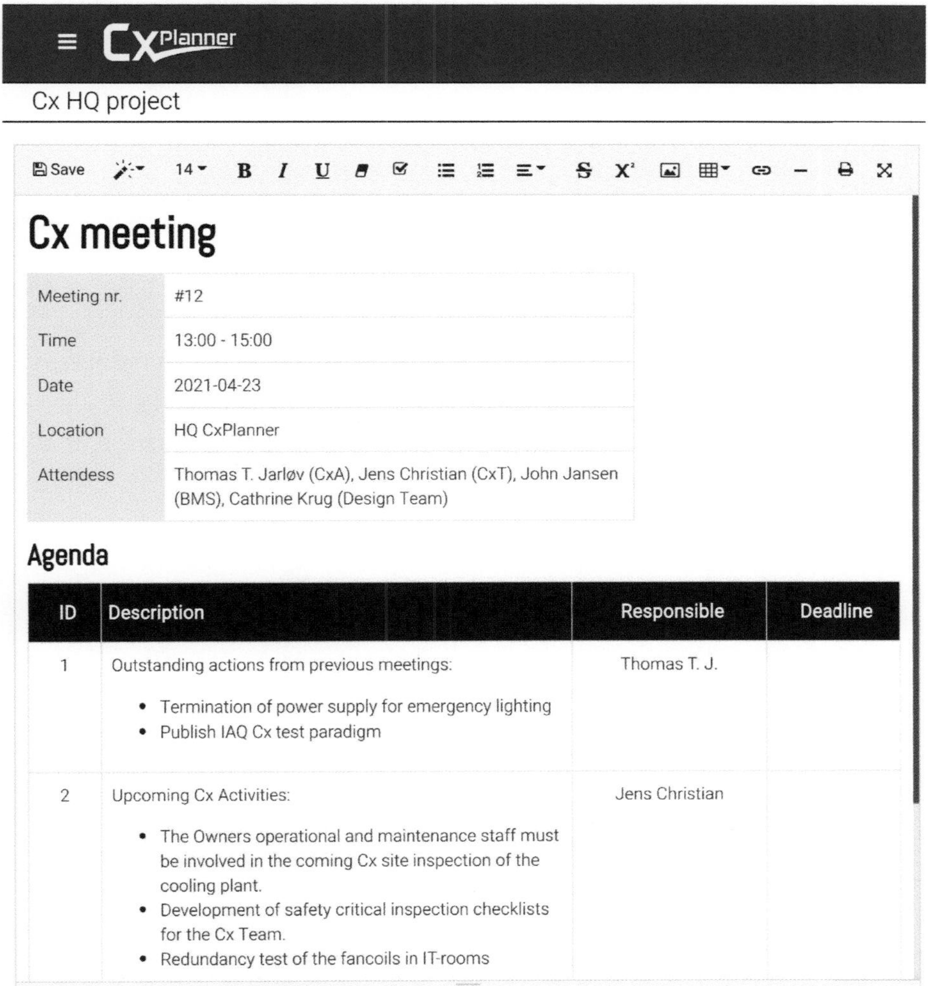

Cx HQ project

Cx meeting

Meeting nr.	#12
Time	13:00 - 15:00
Date	2021-04-23
Location	HQ CxPlanner
Attendess	Thomas T. Jarløv (CxA), Jens Christian (CxT), John Jansen (BMS), Cathrine Krug (Design Team)

Agenda

ID	Description	Responsible	Deadline
1	Outstanding actions from previous meetings: • Termination of power supply for emergency lighting • Publish IAQ Cx test paradigm	Thomas T. J.	
2	Upcoming Cx Activities: • The Owners operational and maintenance staff must be involved in the coming Cx site inspection of the cooling plant. • Development of safety critical inspection checklists for the Cx Team. • Redundancy test of the fancoils in IT-rooms	Jens Christian	

Figure 23. Example of Cx minutes in www.CxPlanner.com

8.8. Commissioning Site Inspection

Requirements from	Perform activity	Prepare document
ASHRAE G0	**Required**	**Required**
ASHRAE STD 202	Not required	Not required
DS 3090	**Required**	**Required**

Cx Site Inspection checklists can be collated with the general site inspection plans. The difference is that Cx Site Inspection checklists are used exclusively by the Cx Team.

8.8.1. Inspection checklist

Inspection checklists must be drawn up and used by the Cx Team for inspections. It is the responsibility of the Cx Provider to ensure that Cx inspection checklists are developed.

If there are observations in the Cx Log or Cx Review Report that can be verified or clarified by site inspections, then the checklists must be updated with them.

The Cx Site Inspection must include the installations set out in section 5.4, "Scope of commissioning process".

8.8.2. First-time inspections

New installations must be inspected directly after they have been set up. If possible, the initial inspections should also be carried out on general installations, such as lighting installations.

The inspections must check the installation, assembly and documentation. On systems with several disciplines involved, such as a ventilation plant, the inspection must also include component checks. For a ventilation plant, this is done by reviewing the installation site for all components and comparing them with the PI-diagram of the system.

Consideration must be given to whether the Cx first-time site inspection can be merged or combined with the general site inspections (section 7.3.2, "First-time inspections").

8.8.3. Example of a Cx Site Inspection checklist

The examples of the Cx Site Inspection checklists below show some of the items that the checklists may contain.

Cx Site Inspection checklist for a ventilation plant	
1	The location of components is consistent with the PI-diagram.
2	Manometers and other reading equipment are set at user-friendly heights (below 190cm and above 120cm) which ensure that O&M staff can read values without aids (e.g. ladders).
3	Hoses for pressure sensors, for example, are secured so that they are not blocked or broken when opening the plants doors.
4	Machine and self-tapping screws are recessed or cut on the inside of the plant so that the O&M staff cannot cut themselves on them.
5	Power supply separators are installed so that the supply to the fans, for example, can be interrupted before the plant doors are opened.
6	There is sufficient free space in front of the plant so that filters and rotary heat exchanger can be replaced without destructive work. This also includes that all doors can be opened without obstruction.
7	Safety signs are mounted on doors and hatches with moving machine parts behind them.

Table 10. Ventilation checklist.

Cx Site Inspection checklist lighting system	
1	At least one luminaire must be dismantled and taken down as a sample. Bracket/assembly must be checked.
2	Safety wire is installed so that the luminaire cannot fall down.
3	The luminaire is labelled according to the project material.
4	The power supply to the luminaire is fixed and mounted correctly.
5	At least one of the luminaires must be powered on and the lux, Ra and Kelvin values must be measured.
6	When powering on, check that there are no black areas in the lighting area on the luminaire (there must be an entire illuminating surface).

Table 11. Lighting checklist.

8.8.4. Including O&M staff in the site inspection

The Owner's O&M organization, if known, must participate in the site inspection. The scope and number of inspections must be adapted to the size of the building, but at least one inspection must include participation of the O&M organization.

It is the O&M staff who will be responsible for the installations after they have been put into service; it is, therefore, important that their input to the installations is collected. If they observe problems, there is an opportunity to resolve these before the building is put into service.

The inspection may be carried out as part of the first-time inspections, but it must be carried out at least 2 weeks before the start of the Cx tests.

8.9. Documentation

Requirements from	Perform activity	Prepare document
ASHRAE G0	**Required**	**Required**
ASHRAE STD 202	**Required**	**Required**
DS 3090	**Required**	**Required**

The documentation requirements are described in section 6.4, “Systems Manual”.

8.9.1. Sample submission

If sample submission is required, the Cx Team must review the delivered material. The Owner’s O&M staff should participate in the review of the O&M material.

8.9.2. Technical dossier

The Cx Team must review the submitted technical dossier documentation for the machinery, paying particular attention to the following documents:

a. Declaration of Conformity

b. Instructions for use in native language

c. Risk assessment (overall risk assessment for combined machinery)

See section 8.14, “Machinery Directive” for more information about the technical dossier and the DoC.

8.9.3. Commissioning documents

On completion of the project, the Cx documentation must be handed over to the Owner. The Cx Provider is responsible for structuring and submitting all Cx documents together.

Cx documents include at least the following, unless otherwise specifically described in the Systems Manual.

a. OPR
b. Cx Plan
c. Cx Log
d. Acceptance documents (phase approval)
e. Basis of Design (BoD)
f. Cx minutes of meetings
g. The Test overview
h. Test paradigms
i. Test reports
j. Training plan
k. Lessons learned
l. Cx Report

8.10. Test paradigms

Requirements from	Perform activity	Prepare document
ASHRAE G0	**Required**	**Required**
ASHRAE STD 202	**Required**	**Required**
DS 3090	**Required**	**Required**

Test paradigms must be drawn up specifying test procedures, conditions for a test can be started and requirements for the outcome of the test. The test paradigms will be completed in the Construction Phase, where they will be updated with observations from the Cx Log. It is recommended that the Cx Team specify requirements for how these tests are performed and documented to ensure an adequate level of quality.

The Cx Provider is responsible for developing the test paradigms. Often, this will require communication with the Design Team, Contractor and suppliers in order to establish the final test procedures. Likewise, the Cx Provider must ensure that all parties involved in the Cx process are informed of what and how to test.

Test paradigms must be drawn up for all areas contained in the Cx process (section 5.4, "Scope of commissioning process").

8.10.1. The Contractor's test paradigms

If the Cx Team has specific additional requirements for the Contractor's test paradigms, these must be specified in the tender documents/contract agreement. Additions to the Contractor's test paradigms could, for example, be requirements for measuring Ra values and the way in which the measurement is documented. See section 8.11.2, "The Contractor's test" for areas where stricter requirements should be set for the Contractor's test paradigms. Similarly, the requirements for the structure of test paradigms in section 8.10.2, "Design of test paradigms" should be used.

8.10.2. Design of test paradigms

The general information must describe the installation being tested, participants in the test, date, time and place. This information should appear on the front page so that it is easy to see what the test paradigm is about.

a. Test Name
b. Installation/system name
c. Type of installation/system
d. Test date
e. Test leader
f. Participants
g. Purpose of the test
h. Instruments and equipment to be used during the test
i. Possible risks and consequential damages

Prerequisites for the test are the elements that must be clarified/approved before the test can be started. These may be requirements for other tests to be carried out and O&M documentation to be submitted.

a. Mechanical and electrical complete
b. Testing, Adjusting and Balancing
c. Tests
d. QA documentation
e. O&M documentation
f. Prior tests

The test procedure specifies exactly how the test should be performed. The procedure must clearly describe how each test element is performed. The description must be comprehensible to persons who have not yet seen the installation.

a. General description of the test

b. Test setup

c. Procedure for performing the individual tests

The acceptance criteria are the requirements for the outcome that must be meet. These can, for example, be specific temperatures in areas or the performance of a cooling unit.

a. Specific acceptance criteria

b. Reference to the relevant OPR item

See section 10.6, "Test paradigm (indoor climate test)" for an example of an indoor climate test paradigm. The test paradigms can also be built in the Cx software www.CxPlanner.com, see Figure 24, "Example of a test paradigm in CxPlanner.".

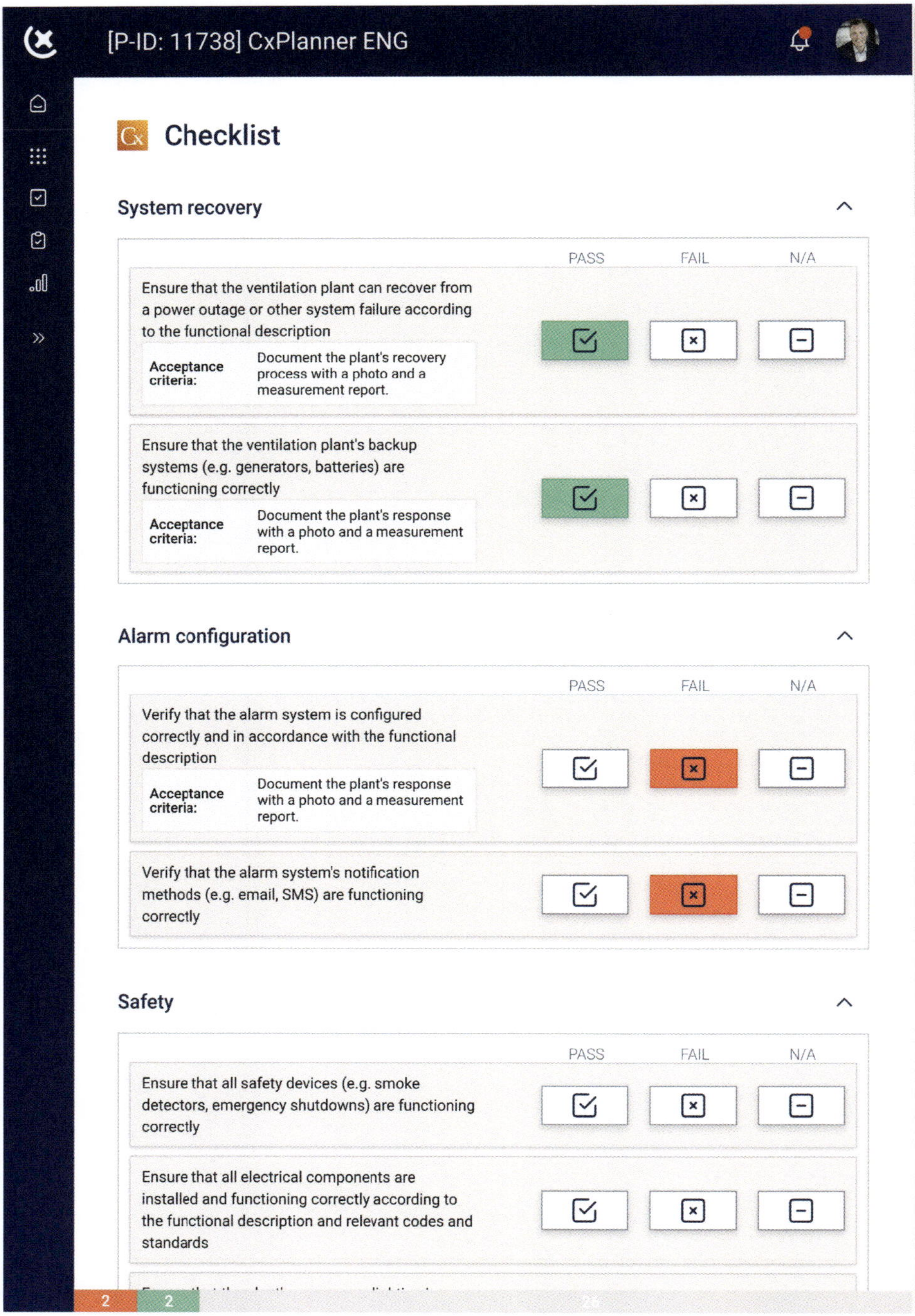

Figure 24. Example of a test paradigm in CxPlanner.

8.11. Test

Requirements from	Perform activity	Prepare document
ASHRAE G0	**Required**	**Required**
ASHRAE STD 202	**Required**	**Required**
DS 3090	**Required**	**Required**

There are several different types of tests, which vary in detail and scope. As a starting point, all tests should be performed according to test paradigms and reported in test reports. The Cx Team must assess how many of the Contractor's tests they wish to participate in.

8.11.1. Prerequisites

The prerequisites for performing a test must always be checked before starting the test.

In general, it should be checked that the plant is mechanical and electrical complete[11] before starting a test, which includes:

a. Components and installations are fully assembled.

b. All switchboards are mounted and on.

c. All electrical connections have been completed and power is applied.

d. All BMS cables are mounted on components and modules.

e. All network cables are routed and connected.

f. All DoC documentation has been submitted.

g. Component and cable marking are completed.

h. Pipe marking is completed.

i. Pipe systems are pressurized and filled.

j. Duct work has been completed and pressure tested.

k. Duct marking is completed.

l. Cable trays are closed when they are going through walls.

[11] Mechanical and electrical complete is based on the Danish Building and Property Agency "Milepæl 2 - Mekanisk og elektrisk komplet".

m. All HMI's (Human Machine Interface) are active.

8.11.2. The Contractor's test

The Contractor's own test is the individual professional Contractor's' testing of their own installations. The test is often described in tender control plans, activated by references to standards and described in the Contractor's own QA plan.

If the Cx Team will adjust and influence the Contractor's test, this must be described in the tender documentation. However, any change to the Contractor's test should take into account the Contractor's certifications, such as *ISO 9001*. Any changes may result in the Contractor having to perform the test in a way that they are not familiar with, resulting in deterioration in quality and increased time taken to adjust the documentation to their *ISO 9001* certification. Therefore, the Cx Team must ensure that the Contractor has the necessary professional competencies if changes are made to the Contractor's tests.

It is recommended that the requirements for the Contractor's test should be improved and detailed for areas where there are no standards describing specific test requirements or where the standard allows the Contractor to choose the test level. These could, for example, be requirements for measuring the Ra and Kelvin values of luminaires, which are not required to be measured according to *DS/EN 12464-1*.

In such an adaptation of the Contractor's test, the Cx Team and the Contractor must collaborate to develop test paradigms, and the Cx Team must monitor the performance of the test itself, as necessary.

The following of the Contractor's self-tests should at least be strengthened:

a. TAB for ventilation.

b. TAB for hydraulic installations (cooling and heating).

c. Measurement of lux, Ra and Kelvin (lighting).

d. Loop tuning/Step Response (BMS).

e. Measurement of lux (emergency and panic lighting).

f. Connected fire protection installations (see section 10.8, "Fire technical system integration test").

8.11.3. Testing requirements from the building code

If the national building code requires specific tests, these should be compared to the planned Cx test. In some cases, they can be combined with the Cx Process.

In Denmark, the Danish Building regulations require functional tests to be carried out on selected technical installations. The requirements are described in *Bygningsreglementet BR18 § 248, § 384, § 391 and § 450*.

The functional tests must be documented in functional test reports to be submitted to the municipality before putting the building into service.

8.11.4. FAT test

Factory Acceptance Test (FAT) is a test that verifies at the supplier's factory/production site that a plant complies with the specifications. The Cx Team must participate in FAT testing and specify test procedure and outcome requirements. Critical installations, such as cooling systems and diesel generators, often have to undergo FAT tests.

The FAT test often consists of three main elements:

a. Inspections (cabling, marking, assembly, etc.).

b. Testing of specifications (water flow, energy consumption, etc.).

c. Functional test (simulated use scenario test).

A FAT test paradigm must always be drawn up containing a detailed description of the test procedure and the outcome requirements. Often, the supplier has a standard FAT test paradigm that can form the basis for the test paradigm.

8.11.5. SAT test

Site Acceptance Test (SAT) is a test that verifies that the plant works in accordance with the requirements when installed at the building site.

The outcome requirements for the SAT test must be described in the OPR. The SAT test will verify all plant functions, such as start-up, shutdown, loading, emergency and fault conditions, energy consumption and alarms.

SAT testing can only be performed after all parts of the plant have been tested and approved. This shmustall include:

a. Completion of the work.
b. Approved FAT test report (if FAT test is required).
c. QA documentation.
d. TAB reports
e. Approved SAT test paradigm.

8.12. Pre-test

Requirements from	Perform activity	Prepare document
ASHRAE G0	Not required	Not required
ASHRAE STD 202	Not required	Not required
DS 3090	Not required	Not required

During the pre-test, the Contractor must verify that installations and systems work in accordance with the project requirements and across disciplines. The test must include the joint testing of several installations with functional coherence. The testing must be carried out and coordinated with all Contractors and suppliers involved in the system.

Pre-test is often referred to as a SIT test. See section 10.9, "Description: Pre-test" for an in-depth description of the pre-test.

8.12.1. Prerequisites for the pre-test

It is a prerequisite that the TAB and testing of installations has been carried out and approved before the pre-test. Approved discipline test reports and all tests, cf. the Contractor's QA systems, must be carried out before the pre-test. This includes pressure tests, adjustments and functional tests.

8.12.2. Participants in the pre-test

Suppliers and Contractors supplying components and installations or involved in constructing the system must provide the necessary resources for participation in the pre-test.

8.12.3. Managing and coordination

In the case of a Turnkey contractor, the concerned Contractor is responsible for the management, planning and coordination of the pre-test. If the Contractor does not have experience or skills to manage the pre-test, the Cx Provider must participate and support the Contractor's test manager.

If the pre-test includes interfaces to the BMS system, the pre-test must be managed by the BMS Contractor, but the Turnkey Contractor remains responsible for the test, including coordination with Contractors from other contracts.

As a rule, the Cx Team does not participate in the pre-test. However, the Cx Team should be able to participate if they consider it necessary. The test dates for the pre-test must be provided to the Cx Team at least 2 weeks before the pre-test itself.

8.12.4. Test paradigm

The Contractor must draw up a test paradigm that shows how the interfaces between the different installations are tested. In some cases, a detailed BMS functional description may form the basis of the test paradigm if this description contains information such as signal types, operating scenarios and the functional cohesion of the controlled installations.

The test paradigm must be approved by the Cx Provider prior to the test.

8.12.5. Test report

Once the pre-test has been performed, a test report must be submitted to the Cx Provider. The test report must contain information on deviations from the test paradigm and must include all measured, visual and calculated values.

It must be made clear whether the installation has passed or failed the test.

The report must, as a minimum, contain:

a. Test leader.
b. Test participants.
c. Date and place of the test.
d. If tests from the test paradigm have not been performed, the reason and justification must be provided.
e. Confirmation that all prerequisites were met before the test was started.
f. All test results must be reported (measured, visual and calculated).
g. Conclusion of the test.

8.13. Training requirements for the O&M staff

Requirements from	Perform activity	Prepare document
ASHRAE G0	**Required**	**Required**
ASHRAE STD 202	**Required**	**Required**
DS 3090	**Required**	**Required**

The Cx Provider must ensure that the training and education requirements for the Owner's O&M organization are identified. The requirements must be reconciled with the type of O&M organization, e.g., internal, outsourced or shared O&M organization.

Relevant training must ensure that O&M personnel are given the appropriate skills to perform day-to-day O&M, as well as the skills to act in the event of failures and emergencies.

8.13.1. Training method

The form of training must be clarified with the O&M staff. The form can be practical review of installations, guidance, e-learning, presentations, etc. The form should be chosen on the basis of the following criteria:

a. Number of operators to participate.

b. Professional background of the operators.

c. Criticality and complexity of installations.

d. How the training is to be carried out when new operators are hired after the building is put into service.

Regardless of the training format chosen, part of the training must be carried out at the current facilities, as theoretical training can then be supported by practical use scenarios.

8.13.2. Training material

The training material must be designed in such a way that it can be reused when new operators are employed.

The training material must include at least the following items:

a. Installation and system structure (sealing off points, etc.).
b. Daily O&M.
c. Replacement of components (sensors on sliding doors, etc.).
d. Control (BMS, HMI on elevators, etc.).
e. Handling of errors (fault codes and how to correct the errors).
f. Management of emergency situations (pipe leakage, overheating in cross field rooms, fire, chemical spillage, etc.).

The Cx Team must review the training material before it is released.

8.13.3. Training plan

The training plan must include:

a. Purpose
b. Attendees
c. Reference to where relevant documentation is available (QA, functional descriptions, As-Built, training material)
d. Review of installation and systems structure
e. Operation
f. Tests after servicing
g. Maintenance
h. Maintenance performed through service contracts
i. Troubleshooting (activities to isolate the fault and fix it)
j. Emergencies (emergency action plans)
k. Contacts

See section 10.5, "Training plan with examples of learning objectives" for an example.

8.13.4. Scheduling the training

The training must be provided during the Construction Phase and, as far as possible, before putting the building into service. However, there may be installations and systems where training is only possible during the actual operational phase, when the end-user uses them. This may be the case with fume cupboards, locks or gate controls.

8.13.5. Evaluation of training

The training must be evaluated by the Cx Team to ensure that the O&M staff have acquired the appropriate competencies. If the O&M staff have not achieved the appropriate level of competence, the training plan must be updated and the training reviewed and repeated.

2-3 weeks after completion of the training, the Cx Team needs to perform a follow-up evaluation. 5-10% of the trainees must participate in a short test, based on questions about subjects that were included in the course.

The Cx Team must select a random installation, and a given number of users among the 5-10% selected must demonstrate that they are familiar with the maintenance of the installation.

8.13.6. Example of elementary training areas

The training must include a review of the specific functions of the installation. A BMS-monitored thermal smoke ventilation could include:

a. Access to BMS screens.

b. Access to BMS functional description.

c. Where the BMS sub-switchboard is located.

d. Where the power supply for the smoke ventilation is located.

e. Description of alarm priorities and any time delays on these.

f. The use scenario for the thermal smoke ventilation.

g. Disconnection of the power supply.

h. Checking the battery backup.

8.14. Machinery Directive

Requirements from	Perform activity	Prepare document
ASHRAE G0	Not required	Not required
ASHRAE STD 202	Not required	Not required
DS 3090	Not required	Not required

The manufacturer of the machinery must be defined for each of the machines. In the case of assembled machines, such as a ventilation plant with BMS, one machinery manufacturer of the assembled machinery must also be defined. The machinery manufacturer has overall responsibility for the machine installation and the associated DoC documentation.

Definition of a machine

> an assembly, fitted with or intended to be fitted with a drive system other than directly applied human or animal effort, consisting of linked parts or components, at least one of which moves, and which are joined together for a specific application.
>
> — Machinery Directive Article 2 (a)

8.14.1. Early submission of DoC documentation

Requirements may be imposed that a supplier may only commence the installation of equipment covered by the DoC requirement after the DoC documentation has been submitted to the Cx Team or the building management and approved. By using this requirement in the contract material with the supplier, it is ensured that the documentation is submitted in a timely manner.

However, the requirement may have an impact on the Cx Team's tasks, as they must check the documentation as soon as possible at the request of the supplier. If the Cx Team does not have the time, there is a risk that the supplier will not be able to start the installation of the machine according to the schedule.

8.14.2. Technical dossier

The technical dossier is the name of the machine documentation containing the essential documentation. The *Machinery Directive's* general requirements for the technical documentations can be found in *Machinery Directive Annex VII Part A*. In addition to the specific requirements for the documentation, there are also requirements for the technical documentation to be available for at least 10 years after the date of manufacture of the machinery.

8.14.3. Declaration of Conformity

A Declaration of Conformity must contain references to the Directives, harmonized standards and standards which the machinery complies with. For example, a Declaration of Conformity for an automatic sliding door should refer to the *Machinery Directive* (because it is a machine) and *EN 16005 Automatic doors – Safety in use – Requirements and test methods*. Pay particular attention to the fact that the reference indicates the year of publication of the Directive or the Standard to ensure that it is the latest version.

8.14.3.1. User manual

The *Machinery Directive's* requirements for the user manual are at the heavy end, which means that there are strict requirements for the content, compared to what many suppliers think they will have to deliver. The *Machinery directive's* requirements for the user manual are listed in *Machinery Directive Appendix 1 section 1.7.4* and related sub-items and include:

a. a general description of the machinery;

b. drawings, diagrams, descriptions and explanations for the use, maintenance and repair of the machinery for checking its correct functioning;

c. a description of the workstation(s) likely to be occupied by operators;

d. instructions for the putting into service and use of the machinery and, if necessary, instructions for the training of operators;

e. instructions on the protective measures to be taken by the user, including, where appropriate, the personal protective equipment to be provided;

8.14.3.2. Risk assessment

Machinery Directive Annex VII A. point 1a, section 4 describes that the technical dossier must include a risk assessment. A risk assessment is a document that describes how the various risks associated with the machine are handled.

If the machine system is a mechanical sliding door, the Declaration of Conformity will often refer to EN 16005, which contains distance requirements to avoid the risk of crushing. In this case, the risk assessment will, among other things, deal with how the risk of squeezing danger has been handled - for example by fitting shielding strips.

The Cx requirements must stipulate that the machine manufacturer must hand over the risk assessment for all plants, as the machine manufacturer is, in principle, not obliged to hand this over. Risk assessments are designed in different levels of detail; for escalators, it may, for example, include the risk assessment of the internal PLC control and electronic components.

It should, therefore, be specified that the submitted risk assessment does not have to include a specific risk assessment of the individual sub-components, such as a risk assessment of the printed circuit board in escalators, but that the risk assessment must be for the functions of the overall machine.

The risk assessment must be performed for the current environment in which the machine is located.

8.14.4. Machine Directive inspection

A Machine Directive inspection of the machine system must be carried out with a satisfactory result before the machine may be commissioned. The Machine Directive inspection must ensure that the machinery has been completed, cf. *Machines Directive*, directives, standards and harmonized standards. This is done by checking the documentation and inspecting the machine.

A Machine Directive inspection can only be carried out when:

a. The following documentation has been approved:

   I. Declaration of Conformity

   II. Instructions for use (manual) in the user's native language

   III. Overall risk assessment

b. The Contractor has completed and checked the installation.

c. All safety functions (e.g., alarms, emergency extraction) are tested and work.

The Machine Directive inspection can be led by a participant from the Cx Team with the right competencies within machine systems. The machine manufacturer must participate in the Machine Directive inspection, and the inspection must be documented and reported to the Cx Provider. The checklist for the Machine Directive inspection can be built in the Cx software www.CxPlanner.com, see Figure 25.

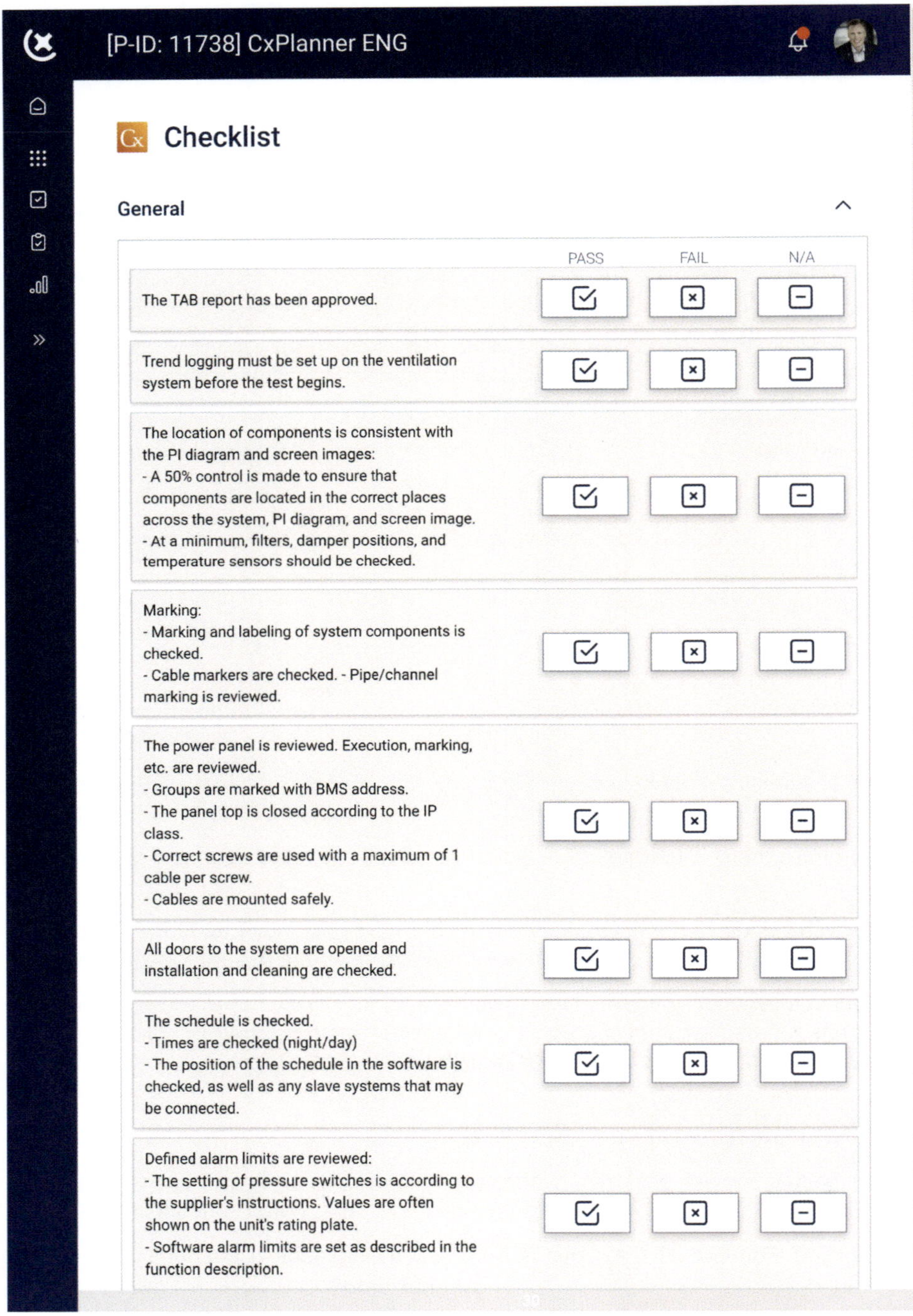

Figure 25. Example of items in a Machine Directive inspection checklist.

8.14.5. Example of items to check during a Machine Directive inspection

During the Machine Directive inspection, the relevant items for the machine system must be checked. Specific items to be controlled must be added for each machine system, depending on the construction and installation location.

Risk assessment	
1	The risk assessment covers the entire machinery. That is, the document includes the assembled system if the machine system includes other sub-components (e.g. ventilation plant and BMS control).
2	The risk assessment is in the native language.
3	The risk assessment describes how the various risks have been removed, mitigated or managed.
4	The risk assessment must be carried out for the installation in question in the area in question.
5	If standards are referred to in the Declaration of Conformity, e.g. EN 16005, the various risks in the standard must be covered. With EN 16005, this will, for example, be a danger of squeezing when the door closes.
6	Are risks assessed with children in mind? This specifically means public areas where children are present. Distance and safety limits are different for children, e.g. EN 13857.
7	The risk assessment must include situations arising from normal use.
8	The risk assessment must include workflows that occur during O&M.

Table 12. Machine Directive: inspection of the risk assessment.

Electrical installation	
1	A final inspection of the electrical installation has been handed in, which documents that the electrical installation has been carried out and complies with national requirements.
2	Supply disconnectors are fitted, which ensure that the voltage supply to the machine system can be interrupted.
3	Supply separators are located visibly and logically in relation to the machine part which they disconnect. The placement height should be between 0.6 and 1.9 meters. There must be a clear and visible cohesion relationship between the machinery and supply separators.
4	All supply separators are marked with a direct association to what they supply, as well as the association with the electrical switchboard.

Electrical installation	
5	Equalizing connections are fitted. This includes a maximum of 1 equalization connection during each fastening and cable trays, machine and metal objects within 2.5 meters are equalized.

Table 13. Machine Directive: inspection of the electrical installations.

Emergency stop	
1	An emergency stop is fitted to the machine system. The emergency stop must be so designed that it is easy for the operator to identify and operate.
2	Emergency stops are located at each control panel, except where this is not necessary according to the risk assessment.
3	The emergency stop can be activated by one hand and is fitted between 0.6 and 1.7 meters above the access level (floor or platform where the operator is located).
2	When activating the emergency stop, all parts of the machine stop.
3	The emergency stop is visible and can be activated with a flat palm.

Table 14. Machine Directive: inspection of the emergency stops.

Risks	
1	There may be unforeseen hazards during starting, stopping or emergency stopping of the machinery.
2	Are there sharp edges, corners, surfaces, tools, etc. that could pose a risk to the system?
3	Is there a risk of being locked inside the machine system, e.g., in connection with service?
4	Is there electrical, hydraulic, pneumatic or other energy that may pose a risk, e.g., during service, due to stored energy?
5	The efficiency of the guards for the machine system is solid, designed so that it is not possible to climb on them, resistant, ensures sufficient transparency and complies with safety distances; for example, for rotating parts, such as fans and belt drives.
6	Fixed guards are attached, so it is necessary to use tools to remove or open them.
7	Necessary measures have been taken to secure against the risk of crushing. For example, distance between moving door leaf and wall.
8	Fall protection has been established at the machine plant; for example, railings or fall belts at heights of more than 500mm.

Table 15. Machine Directive: inspection of the risks.

8.15. Commissioning test (SIT)

Requirements from	Perform activity	Prepare document
ASHRAE G0	**Required**	**Required**
ASHRAE STD 202	**Required**	**Required**
DS 3090	**Required**	**Required**

The Cx test is the final test which verifies that the systems comply with the Cx requirements. The Cx test is often called a SIT test.

Some Cx tests require specific seasonal conditions or that the building is in use before the test can be performed - including indoor climate tests. In these tests, the Cx Team must assess whether it is possible to simulate such assumptions; heat load can, for example, be simulated using fan heaters. If it is not possible to obtain correct conditions, the Cx test must be postponed until this is possible, see section 9.2, "Loaded and seasonal tests" for stress- and seasonal-tests.

See section 10.10, "Description: Cx test" for an in-depth description of the Cx-test.

8.15.1. System Integration Test

The Cx test includes systems where several plants, installations and disciplines are interconnected directly or indirectly, or where the functions of several plants are used together. For example, a ventilation system often consists of several different installations and disciplines, which is why a system integration test is necessary. Likewise, a Cx test of the indoor climate must also be performed, where several different systems together ensure that the indoor climate complies with the Cx requirements.

Often, there are many parameters that affect systems. Figure 26 shows several different parameters that influence the indoor climate. Some of the parameters are directly connected, such as the ventilation and BMS system, while user influence indirectly affects the indoor climate.

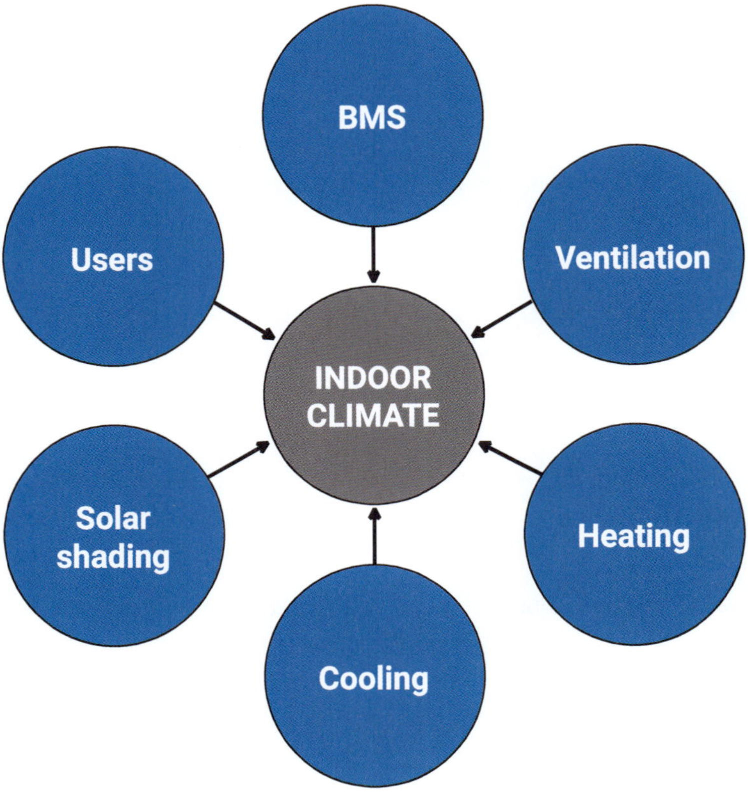

Figure 26. Elements that has influence on the indoor climate.

8.15.2. Scope of testing

Cx tests must be performed on all installations specified in section 5.4, “Scope of commissioning process”. Cx tests should also be performed on business-critical systems and on fire technical installations, cf. the fire strategy (see section 10.8, “Fire technical system integration test”).

The individual tests should include:

a. Personal and machine safety.

b. Component integrations (BMS control of valves, etc.).

c. Functions and signal transmissions across systems and disciplines.

d. Control and regulation.

e. Performance and load tests.

f. Error and emergency scenarios.

8.15.2.1. Reserve supply (UPS system and diesel generator)

Reserve supply systems must ensure that the supply to facilities is maintained in the event of a power failure. The backup supply often consists of both battery backup (UPS) and diesel generators.

An example of a Cx test of the backup supply could be if the company’s server center is supplied by both a UPS system and a diesel generator, while the company’s production line is only supplied by the diesel generator. The Cx test must, in this case, verify that in the event of a power failure there is no failure on the server center, as it is UPS-supplied, while there will be a failure on the production line until the diesel generator is started up.

A controlled power failure is performed:

a. Server central, provided with both UPS system and diesel generator, continues without outage.

b. Production line supplied only by diesel generator stops due to power failure and restarts when the diesel generator is started up.

c. Alarm signals are transmitted to the Owner’s operation center.

The power is switched on again:

a. The server center continues its operation without failure.

b. The production line continues its operation without outage.

c. Alarm signals are transmitted to the Owner's operation center.

8.15.2.2. Indoor climate

The indoor climate in buildings is often governed by many parameters, as well as the specific season. The ventilation system ensures, for example, an air exchange, which is based on parameters from the BMS system's temperature and CO_2 sensors.

The Cx test must verify that the integration and regulation of these plants works, cf. OPR.

The indoor climate is logged for a period of 20 days:

a. The operating temperature and CO_2 level meet the Cx requirements.

b. In the event of any deviations from temperature and the CO_2 requirements, it is checked by logging from window and door contacts whether windows and doors have been opened.

c. There has been a stable regulation throughout the 20 days without commuting of heating and cooling valves.

8.15.3. Management and coordination of the test

The Cx test must be managed and coordinated by the Cx Team. All the Contractor's responsible resources for installations that are part of the overall system must participate in the test.

The individual from the Design Team who designed the specific system must attend. For systems managed by BMS, in some cases it will be sufficient for only the BMS Contractor to participate.

8.15.4. Prerequisites

Before a Cx test can be performed, the following prerequisites must be met:

a. The system is mechanically and electrically complete (section 8.11.1, "Prerequisites")

b. All tests, cf. the Contractor's QA system, must be performed.

c. All QA material must be available (redlines is accepted).

d. O&M documentation must be available (redlines accepted).

e. BMS screens must be reviewed and approved.

f. BMS function descriptions and BMS board drawings are As-Built and approved.

g. All tests cf. legislation must be performed.

h. All tests cf. applicable standards must be performed, e.g., adjustments and testing.

i. All documentation cf. applicable standards must be available (redlines accepted).

j. The Contractors have carried out pre-tests which demonstrate that the functions for each individual discipline and across the disciplines meet the project requirements and that there is documentation for this.

k. Other work must be carried out in such a way that its completion does not in any way prevent or influence the Cx test.

8.15.5. Test paradigm

The Cx Provider must prepare the test paradigm for the Cx test. If the Contractor's test paradigm from the pre-test is adequate, the Cx Provider can use this as a basis for the test paradigm.

The test paradigm must at least include:

a. Description of the system.

b. The purpose of the test.

c. Risk analysis (mitigating actions).

d. Participants in the Cx Test.

e. Prerequisite list (see section 10.7, “Test requirements”).

f. Test equipment and calibration requirements.

g. Diagrams and process diagrams.

h. Acceptance requirements.

The functional descriptions of the BMS system can be used in connection with the preparation of the test paradigms. Function descriptions often contain concrete descriptions of the system’s functions and reaction patterns, which the individual test procedures may include as verification parameters.

8.15.6. Test report

The test report must contain the items from the test paradigm and as a minimum:

a. The results for each test procedure.

b. Any deviations from test procedure.

c. Conclusion - rejection or approval of test.

8.16. Lessons learned

Requirements from	Perform activity	Prepare document
ASHRAE G0	**Required**	Not required
ASHRAE STD 202	Not required	Not required
DS 3090	Not required	Not required

The Lessons Learned session is the evaluation of the Cx process, which is designed to result in specific recommendations to the project participants for use in their next project with Cx. If a general Lessons Learned session is already being held on the project, Cx as a topic can often be included in this.

In cases where it is not possible to hold the Lessons Learned session in the Construction Phase, the session is moved to the Occupancy and Operation phase. There is often a great deal of activity on the construction site during the handover, which may mean that not everyone has the opportunity to participate.

All participants in the Cx process must participate in the Lessons Learned session, so that all points of view and experiences are reviewed. The Cx Provider is responsible for the management and coordination. The form and structure of the session must be agreed with the Owner.

8.16.1. Form

The form must be adapted to the professional level of the participants and to the size and complexity of the project. Subject-specific meetings, workshops, interviews, questionnaires, etc. can be held. There is a big difference in how much time the different methods require. Often a workshop requires more time than a questionnaire survey.

Common to the various forms is that they must analyze constructive and concrete examples. If there have been incidents in the project which have resulted in financial losses for one or more parties, but which are irrelevant for the Cx process, these must not be included.

8.16.2. Structure

The content of the Lessons Learned session must focus on all the parties involved:

a. Owner

b. Design Team

c. Contractor

d. Subcontractors

e. The Cx Team

The Cx Activities performed must be reviewed, and improvement proposals must result in concrete recommendations that can be implemented. For each of the parties, there must be an evaluation of what they did well and what did not work.

See section 10.11, "Questionnaire for lessons learned" for an example of a questionnaire.

8.17. Cost-benefit

Requirements from	Perform activity	Prepare document
ASHRAE G0	Not required	Not required
ASHRAE STD 202	Not required	Not required
DS 3090	Not required	Not required

A cost-benefit analysis should be prepared of the Cx process, which documents whether it has brought an economic benefit. There is no recognized standardized method for performing cost-benefit analyses over the Cx process: this section, therefore, contains several examples of how different calculation methods can be used.

8.17.1. Saved hours

Cx often means that the various parties on the projects have to spend fewer hours performing their tasks. The hours saved can be capitalized as savings, with a direct attribution to the Cx Activities performed. Often this saving can be divided into:

Parameters	Contents
Coordination	Coordination of the Cx Team between the various actors in the project. This can be by reviewing log items, Cx meetings and joint site inspections.
Test	Checking test conditions and performing tests.
Documentation	Management of documentation control and submission of documentation to the Systems Manual.

Table 16. Categorization of savings by Cx.

An example of a saving could be:

a. The Contractor has reported ready to perform a Cx test, but the Cx Team finds that the test prerequisites have not been met and cancels the test. If the Cx Team had not cancelled the test, the Cx Team and the Owner's O&M staff would have spent *X* hours testing a system that was not ready for testing.

b. At Cx meetings, the interfaces between the various subcontractors were reviewed and errors were found in the interface between the BMS and ventilation. Supplied dampers were to be controlled with a 4-20mA signal, while the BMS contractor expected the dampers to be controlled with a 0-10V signal. Without Cx, the BMS contractor would have spent *X* hours changing this subsequently if the wrong damper was installed.

Hours saved can also be calculated based on the Owner's historical data. This can be done with advantage if the Owner has an internal O&M organization. An example could be:

a. Operating personnel were usually called in for re-testing of ventilation systems up to 10 times, as there were so many errors in the tests that the test was scrapped. The Cx Team has, therefore, had extra focus on verification of ventilation systems. As a result, when the operating personnel were called in for testing of ventilation systems, the test was approved at the first attempt. This results in a 9-re-test, saving multiplied by *X* number of hours.

Figure 27 shows a simple calculation model based on the number of tests held. The calculation model shows the financial costs for testing at: **"Test without Cx"** and **"Test with Cx"**.

				Participants				
	Number of tests	Hour / test	EUR / hour	O&M staff	Contractor	Design Team	Cx Team	Total
Test without Cx	3	5	150	2	1	1	1	25.000 EUR
Test with Cx	1	5	150	2	1	1	1	75.000 EUR
								50.000 EUR

Figure 27. Cost-benefit calculation model for tests performed. The saving is indicated in the green field at the bottom right.

8.17.2. Review savings

Cx also often leads to large savings during the Cx Design Review, where interdisciplinary project errors are discovered. The calculation of these savings is associated with some uncertainty, as one can not disprove that the Design Team or Contractor himself would have found the errors; however, this would have been later in the project.

Figure 28 shows a simple calculation model based on the number of errors found during the Cx Design Review and the economics of the individual review comments.

	Review comments			
	150 EUR	1.500 EUR	3.000 EUR	Total
Pre-Design	50	5	-	100.000 EUR
Schematic Design	100	10	-	200.000 EUR
Design Development	150	15	-	300.000 EUR
Construction Documents	250	20	10	700.000 EUR
				1.300.000 EUR

Figure 28. Cost-benefit calculation model for review comments. The saving is indicated in the green field at the bottom right.

The calculation model can be further detailed with the parameters below:

Parameters	Contents
Time	The time when the error would have been detected if the Cx Team had not found it. The time can be divided into four main groups: - During design - During execution - In the subsequent phase - Never The time has a direct influence on which of the other calculation parameters can be used.
Direct repair costs	The direct cost of fixing the error. There are three cost centers: - Redesign - Working hours for repair (e.g. changing valve) - Product costs (purchase of new valve)
Indirect repair costs	Indirect costs of the repair are downtime and changes in employees' workflows. - Production loss due to closed production line. - Employees cannot perform work process as *X* tool does not work. - Craftsmen must have access to the facilities and be escorted around.
Direct costs incurred	The costs involved include: - Increased energy consumption (e.g. incorrect balancing). - Increased O&M costs (the system often requires inspection or reports faults more often). - Shortened component lifetime (if systems oscillate, the mechanical part components are used more often).
Indirect costs	Decreased productivity due to poor indoor climate (with increased CO_2 level, the staff's ability to concentrate is reduced[12])

[12] REHVA Guidebook 6 & 10

Parameters	Contents
Uncertainty	Any uncertainties must be included. If the error is found by the Cx Team in the project proposal phase, the uncertainty must include: - The Design Team had discovered it in the main project phase. - The site inspection had discovered it during the execution. - The Contractor had discovered it during execution.

Table 17. Parameters used to detail the cost-benefit calculation model.

8.17.3. Derivative benefits

Derivative benefits are calculated as processes and works that are not specific to the Cx Activities, but which have been optimized due to the Cx process. For example, it could be:

a. Combination of the Owner's design review and Cx Design Review.

b. Coordination of the Design Team's site inspection and the Cx site inspection.

c. Documentation flow.

d. Steering group reports and Cx progress reporting.

8.18. Commissioning Report

Requirements from	Perform activity	Prepare document
ASHRAE G0	**Required**	**Required**
ASHRAE STD 202	**Required**	**Required**
DS 3090	**Required**	**Required**

The Cx Report is the final report of the Cx process performed. The Cx Report contains the full documentation of the Cx Activities performed and the final Cx documents.

8.18.1. Structure

The report must include the following:

a. OPR

b. Cx Log

c. Test results

d. Deferred tests

e. Cx Progress Reports

f. Lessons learned

g. Cost-benefit

8.18.2. OPR

The section on the OPR is a summary of the work with the OPR. There must be special focus on the requirements that either could not be met or the requirements that have not yet been met.

The OPR-document must be attached to the Cx Report.

8.18.3. The commissioning log

Any outstanding log items must be listed and an action plan must be specified for how open items are to be closed.

The Cx Log must be attached to the Cx Report.

8.18.4. Test results

An adequate summary of the tests performed and their results must be included. If there are outstanding tests, an action plan must be drawn up which clearly specifies when they can be carried out.

The Test overview can be attached to this section, as it contains a complete overview of all tests performed as well as their results.

8.18.5. Deferred tests

Postponed tests can be tests that require a specific season or load that is not available before the end of the project. The Cx Report must include a full listing of these and an indication of when they are to be performed.

8.18.6. Commissioning Progress reports

The Cx Report must include a summary of the Cx Progress Reports. This is done by including all the Cx Progress Reports or a general summary.

8.18.7. Lessons learned

The section on gathering experience should function as a tool that the Owner can use on other projects with Cx. The section must include the full result from the lessons learned as well as a list of the specific recommendations to the Owner.

8.18.8. Cost-benefit

The results of the cost-benefit analysis must be included and compared against the cost of Cx.

8.19. Update Cx documents

Requirements from	Perform activity	Prepare document
ASHRAE G0	Not required	Not required
ASHRAE STD 202	Not required	Not required
DS 3090	**Required**	Not required

All Cx documents must be updated with the latest information if this has not been carried out during the Construction Phase.

8.19.1. The Commissioning Plan

At the end of the Construction Phase, the Cx Provider must update the Cx Plan with descriptions of the upcoming Cx Activities in the Occupancy and Operations Phase and activities contained in the Ongoing Cx. The update must, as a minimum, describe the following activities in the Occupancy and Operations Phase:

a. Loaded and seasonal tests

b. 10 month review

c. 1-year review

d. Ongoing Cx Plan

8.19.2. Systems Manual

The Systems Manual must be updated with the documentation submitted by the Design Team and the Contractor.

8.20. Phase acceptance

Requirements from	Perform activity	Prepare document
ASHRAE G0	**Required**	**Required**
ASHRAE STD 202	Not required	Not required
DS 3090	**Required**	**Required**

The Owner must approve in writing that the Cx process can continue. The Cx Report must be attached to this phase approval.

The requirements for the acceptance document are set out in section 5.10, "Phase acceptance".

9. Occupancy and Operations Phase

The Occupancy and Operations Phase is started when the construction has been handed over to the Owner. This is when the Owner has started to use the building.

In the Occupancy and Operations Phase, tests must be performed that require specific prerequisites. 10 months after the construction is handed over, a 10-month review must be carried out, which is led by the Cx Provider. This review must verify that plants and systems still comply with the OPR.

After the 10-month review, a follow-up Lessons Learned session must be held, where the O&M staff's experiences with the building in the first 10 months are mapped. This session should update the results of the Lessons Learned session from the Construction Phase.

The Cx Plan must be updated with a description of what a possible ongoing Cx process should be like. The ongoing Cx process must ensure that the functions and regulations of plants and systems are continuously checked. There must be a plan for how the Owner can continuously check that the building's energy consumption is minimized or at least maintained at a low level.

9.1. Commissioning activities

Activity	Document	Description
Stress- and seasonal test	Test paradigm & reports	Tests which rely on a specific load or season are carried out.
10 month inspection	Inspection report	The 10 month inspections of the facility are performed, where OPR items are checked.
Lessons learned	Recommendation report	A second Lessons learned workshop is performed, where operational experience is included.
1 year inspection	Inspection report	1 year after the handover, a final inspection of the facility is performed.
Update Cx documents	Cx documents	All Cx documents must be updated, with decisions and details.
Phase acceptance	Acceptance document	The Owner must approve the performed Cx Activities, and that the ongoing Cx Process can be started.

9.2. Loaded and seasonal tests

Requirements from	Perform activity	Prepare document
ASHRAE G0	**Required**	Not required
ASHRAE STD 202	**Required**	Not required
DS 3090	**Required**	Not required

The loaded and seasonal tests require specific prerequisites that could not be provided during the Construction Phase.

Seasonal tests are characterized by the fact that a specific season is required to ensure the right conditions for the test. For example, the test of a cooling system will require warmer outdoor temperatures, which are only present during a summer period.

Loaded tests require specific loads that are only available when the building is in operation; for example, that a given number of users are using the building and its facilities at the same time.

In some cases, seasonal and load conditions can be achieved by a simulation. A simulation of heat load can be performed, for example, by setting up heating fans, which correspond to the required heating effect.

The tests must be performed as described in section 8.11, “Test”.

9.2.1. Cooling and heating systems

When testing cooling and heating systems, the systems must emit their produced power (cooling or heating). If a cooling system is tested in the winter, there may be a risk that the system's capacity cannot be tested, as there is not the necessary heat load so that the system can emit the projected amount of cooling. The opposite is the case for a heating system that must be tested in a winter season, when heat is needed.

9.2.2. Indoor climate

The indoor climate in a building is dependent on the season; therefore, the indoor climate must be tested in both a summer and winter period. Likewise, the indoor climate is also often dependent on the number of users who use the building. Simulations can be made of both the season and the number of users, by installing heating fans or by overriding heating and cooling valves.

9.2.3. Emergency power supply

When testing the emergency power supply, it is required that all systems supplied by the emergency power supply system are in operation and loaded. It may be, for example, a server center that is connected and emergency supplied with batteries (UPS system) and a diesel generator system. Here, a test must be performed that, when the main power supply is disconnected, the UPS system is activated and the diesel generator is activated afterwards.

9.2.4. Thermography

Thermography of electrical panels requires that the electrical panels are in operation and loaded and that the room temperatures are in a range corresponding to normal operation. It is only when the electrical panels are loaded that a thermography can make any problems visible.

9.3. 10 month inspection

Requirements from	Perform activity	Prepare document
ASHRAE G0	Not required	Not required
ASHRAE STD 202	Not required	Not required
DS 3090	**Required**	Not required

10 months after the delivery of the construction, the Cx Team must perform a 10-month inspection. This inspection is an evaluation and performance check to ensure that the construction still meets the OPR. The Owner can also use the observations in connection with the 1-year inspection.

9.3.1. Coordination of the inspection

It is the Cx Provider who is responsible for convening and managing the inspection with the Cx Team. The inspection should include:

a. Evaluation of the operation with the Owner and the O&M staff.

b. Status of ongoing Cx Activities.

c. Checking setpoints and system settings.

d. Performing energy and performance tests.

9.4. Lessons learned

A follow-up Lessons Learned session should be carried out, based on the O&M organization's experience from the first 10 months of operation.

See section 8.16, "Lessons learned" for method and requirements for performing the lessons learned.

9.5. 1 year inspection

Requirements from	Perform activity	Prepare document
ASHRAE G0	Not required	Not required
ASHRAE STD 202	Not required	Not required
DS 3090	Not required	Not required

The Cx Provider must submit focus items from the Cx process to the Owner, who can use them in the 1 year inspection. It includes items from the Cx Log, Lessons Learned, load tests and seasonal tests.

It is important that, if errors are observed before the 1 year inspection, these must always be reported to the Owner immediately.

9.6. Update Cx documents

Requirements from	Perform activity	Prepare document
ASHRAE G0	**Required**	Not required
ASHRAE STD 202	**Required**	Not required
DS 3090	**Required**	Not required

All Cx documents must be updated with the latest information if this has not been carried out during the Occupancy and Operations Phase. If there are outstanding Cx observations, action plans must be drawn up for them.

9.6.1. Ongoing Cx

Ongoing Cx is a term for Cx Activities that continue during the Occupancy and Operations Phase. Ongoing Cx must ensure that the Owner and the operating staff have the necessary tools for ongoing verification of the facilities.

In ongoing Cx, there is a special focus on monitoring the building's energy consumption. If it is identified that the energy consumption deviates from the expected usage, corrective measures can be implemented immediately.

The Cx Plan must be updated with descriptions of how the ongoing Cx can be performed. It must be ensured that the Owner and the O&M staff can continue to use the Cx tools in the operations, which includes, among other things:

a. Action plans for outstanding OPR items.

b. Managing of the Cx Log.

c. Maintenance of the Systems Manual.

d. Data collection and processing (primarily energy-related data).

e. Testing of plants and systems and performance test.

9.6.2. Commissioning report

The Cx Report must be updated with data from the Occupancy and Operations Phase. It includes test results, the updated collection of experience and observations from the 10-month review.

9.7. Acceptance of the Cx process

Requirements from	Perform activity	Prepare document
ASHRAE G0	**Required**	**Required**
ASHRAE STD 202	Not required	Not required
DS 3090	**Required**	**Required**

The Owner must approve in writing that the Cx process can continue as an ongoing Cx process as described in the Cx Plan. The Cx Report must be attached to the acceptance document.

The requirements for the acceptance document are set out in section 5.10, “Phase acceptance”.

10. Annex

10.1. Cx Activity Matrix

Pre-Design

Cx Activity	Input from	Responsible	Approver	Used by
Roles & responsibility	Owner, CxP	CxP	Owner	Owner
Scope of the Cx Process	Owner, CxP	CxP	Owner	CxP
OPR	Owner, CxP, O&M staff, users	Owner, CxP	Owner	CxP, Design Team
Cx Plan	Owner, CxP, Design Team	CxP	Owner	CxP, Design Team
Start-up meeting	CxP	CxP	Design Team	CxP
Cx Log	Owner, CxP, Design Team	CxP	CxP	Owner, CxP, Design Team
Cx Design Review	CxP	CxP	Owner, Design Team	Design Team
Phase acceptance	CxP	CxP	Owner	Owner

*** CxP = Cx Provider**

Design Development

Cx Activity	Input from	Responsible	Approver	Used by
Start-up meeting	CxP	CxP	Design Team	Design Team
Basis of Design	Design Team	Design Team	CxP	CxP
Systems Manual	Owner, CxP	CxP	Owner	Design Team
Cx Design Review	CxP	CxP	Owner	Design Team
Update Cx documents	CxP	CxP	CxP	CxP
Phase acceptance	CxP	CxP	Owner	Owner

*** CxP = Cx Provider**

Construction Documents

Cx Activity	Input from	Responsible	Approver	Used by
Start-up meeting	CxP	CxP	Design Team	Design Team
Site inspection	CxP, Design Team	Design Team	Owner	CxP, Design Team
Test overview	Design Team	Design Team	CxP	CxP
Test schedule	Design Team	Design Team	CxP	CxP
Requirements to the Contractor	CxP	CxP	Owner	Contractor
Cx Design Review	CxP	CxP	Owner	Design Team
Update Cx documents	CxP	CxP	CxP	CxP
Phase acceptance	CxP	CxP	Owner	Owner

*** CxP = Cx Provider**

Construction phase

Cx Activity	Input from	Responsible	Approver	Used by
Start-up meeting	CxP	CxP	Contractor	Contractor
Cx Progress Reports	CxP	CxP	Owner	Owner
Design made by Contractor	CxP	CxP	Owner, Contractor	Contractor
Test overview	CxP, Contractor	CxP	CxP	CxP, Contractor
Test schedule	Contractor	Contractor	CxP	CxP, Contractor
Cx meetings	CxP, Design Team, Contractor	CxP	CxP	CxP, Design Team, Contractor
Cx Site Inspection	CxP	CxP	Owner	CxP
Documentation	Contractor	Contractor	CxP	CxP
Test paradigms	CxP, Contractor	Contractor	CxP	Contractor
Test	CxP, Design Team, Contractor	CxP, Contractor	CxP	CxP, Contractor
Pre-test	Design Team, Contractor	Contractor	CxP	Contractor, Design Team
Training of O&M staff	Contractor	Contractor	Owner	Owner, CxP

Machinery Directive	CxP, Design Team, Contractor	CxP	Owner	CxP
Cx test	CxP, Design Team, Contractor	CxP	CxP	CxP
Lessons learned	CxP, Design Team, Contractor	CxP	Owner	Owner
Cost-benefit	CxP, Design Team, Contractor	CxP	Owner	Owner
Cx Report	CxP	CxP	Owner	Owner
Update Cx documents	CxP	CxP	CxP	CxP
Phase acceptance	CxP	CxP	Owner	Owner

*** CxP = Cx Provider**

Occupancy and Operations phase

Cx Activity	Input from	Responsible	Approver	Used by
Stress and seasonal test	CxP, Design Team, Contractor	CxP	CxP	CxP, Contractor
10 months inspection	Owner	CxP	Owner	Owner
Lessons learned	Owner, CxP, O&M staff, users	CxP	Owner	Owner
1 year inspection	CxP	Owner	Owner	Owner
Update Cx documents	CxP	CxP	CxP	CxP
Phase acceptance	CxP	CxP	Owner	Owner

*** CxP = Cx Provider**

10.2. OPR: Exemption application

OPR reference	ID: 109
OPR item description	All manometers and monitoring components on ventilation systems may be placed a maximum of 190 centimeters above floor.
BoD	When ordering the ventilation plant, a requirement is stated that components must be placed at a maximum of 190 centimeters above the floor
Dispensation applicant	Thomas T. Jarløv
Date of application	2021-01-01
Justification for application	The ventilation plants will be ordered from Germany. The plant's production line is locked unless a specific change to the product line is purchased. General monitoring components are placed a maximum of 190 centimeters above the floor, as these are components supplied by the BMS contractor. Manometers are part of the supplier's standard components and are always mounted on top of the systems (approximately 180 centimeters above the floor). Due to the high demand for air exchange and the small technical rooms, the ventilation systems must be twice as high (2 placed on top of each other). This means that manometers in the upper system are mounted 240 centimeters above the floor. Monitoring components are installed at a maximum height of 190 centimeters above the floor, which replaces the factory-fitted manometers. The factory-fitted ones are therefore superfluous.
Economy	If the Owner wants the redundant manometers removed from all ventilation systems, 3 solutions can be selected. Solution 1: Change of production line corresponding to approximately 7.000 EUR. Solution 2: Disassemble manometers and close holes about 2.000 EUR. Solution 3: Retention of redundant manometers corresponding to 0 EUR.
Consequences	The various solution proposals do not have consequences for the Owner's O&M staff or the energy consumption. However, solution 1 and 2 have an economic consequence.
Cx Provider's recommendation	The Cx Provider assesses that solution 3 should be chosen. The solution allows for redundant check of subsequently mounted manometers.
O&M staff's recommendation	The Owner's O&M staff has confirmed that they can accept all of solution proposals (1, 2 or 3).

10.3. The OPR document

Below are listed OPR items within 11 technical areas. The OPR items are all requirements that are structured with measurable parameters. The requirements can either be used directly in a Cx process or as inspiration when the Cx Provider has to facilitate the preparation of the Owner's Project Requirements.

10.3.1. Lighting

Lighting
If light sources can be replaced, this must be possible for the O&M staff and not be reserved for the manufacturer. The Declaration of Conformity must not cease if replacement is carried out by O&M staff.
It must be possible to dust the luminaire and reflectors off without dismantling parts of the luminaire.
Luminaires and light source must at least be able to withstand the defined ambient temperatures in the indoor climate +/- 5 C without affecting the performance and/or service life of the luminaire.
Dimmable luminaires must be able to be dimmed continuously from 0 to 100% of full illuminance.
Lighting must be adjusted after furniture is installed in the building. This balancing must be documented by documenting measuring points and values on a floor plan and diagram.
Measurements of lux, Ra and Kelvin values must be made.
The lighting must be able to regulate in relation to the effects of daylight in all zones.
There must be a control system which ensures lighting in the presence of people and switches off the light when it is empty. (The light control must not switch off when people are doing sedentary work).
It must be ensured that a constant lux value is maintained at permanent workplaces, regardless of their location and sunlight.
It must be possible for users to override the lighting in meeting rooms.
Luxmeter used for balancing must have an accuracy of at least 1% (10 - 150,000 lux), 0.1 lux (0.1 - 10 lux).

10.3.2. BMS

BMS
The BMS system must be fully integrated with the Owner's current BMS system. When the operator navigates from the Owner's current BMS system to the new BMS system, e.g. from a system image, it must be possible to do so with 1 click without delay. All signals, alarms and time programs must have a smooth transition and be fully accessible with the same interface.
Alarms must be able to be sent to the Owner's operating staff within normal working hours, and outside normal working hours to external operator. Alarms must be able to be sent both as SMS and email depending on the priority of the alarm.
It must be possible to access the BMS system from anywhere via the Internet, so that all computers in the Owner's organization can be used.
BMS switchboards must be blue and in a metallic surface. They must be marked with a laser engraved sign with a white background and black text and the text must be 30 mm high.
Systems connected to the BMS system must have automatic restart after a power failure and start-up in the last operating mode for all system types.
The BMS system must have a real-time overview of all system parameters - pressure, flow, temperature, energy consumption, load factor, COP, system COP, etc.
O&M staff must have real-time access to data relevant to the operation and troubleshooting of cooling, heating and ventilation systems. This includes all settings, opening degrees, offsets, feedback, etc.
The BMS system must be able to perform data logging at all measuring points connected to the BMS system, so that the operating staff can continuously validate the building's performance.
Step-response tests must be performed on all control loops, which demonstrate that these are stable and fast, and that they stably find a new reference value.
Step response curves should be submitted as graphs with descriptive text of what the components include. If the test includes several components, all of these must be stated (e.g., heating valve, cooling valve, supply pressure and temperature).
The function description must describe how components work, as well as the selected setting parameters (pressure, setpoints, etc.) that are applicable at delivery.
Alarms must be divided into three priorities and support the Owner's alarm level.
It must be possible to group alarms in different areas/system types/categories, etc.
The installation must be designed with 35% extra capacity in the sub-switchboard for each point type, AI, DI, AO, DO and bus, both physically and in program/software.
All technical systems must be controlled, regulated and monitored by the BMS system.

BMS
It must be possible to replace system components without disassembly of fixed installations.
Fire dampers must be able to be tested from the CTS system and a weekly test must be arranged, so that it does not interfere with the daily operation of the building.
Components located behind/above the limb/plate must be visibly marked on the limb/plate and drawings.
The BMS system must be designed in such a way that it can be part of a BMS strategy without locking that strategy on products or solutions.
It must be possible to convert large-scale zones via the BMS system for internal relocations and conversions.
It must be ensured that the BMS system as a whole can be serviced by a single supplier.
The indoor climate must be regulated based on presence detectors, temperature and CO_2 level as an overall regulation.
Room temperatures must be visible in each zone.
It must be possible to set room temperatures in each zone.
All HW points, as well as setpoints and other software points that can be operated, must be visible on graphic images and must be logged. This also applies to systems in zones, e.g. IBI systems.
Humidity sensors must be placed in the building at strategic locations for monitoring, including at the bottom of shafts and in all intersection spaces.
A common ID code system specified in the *XX* must be used for labelling.

10.3.3. Electrical installations

Electrical installations
Electrical installations must be future-proofed with 25% oversizing of cables (both high and low current), cable trays, switchboards and switchboards.
Installation equipment and cables must be lead and PVC free and otherwise support the Owner's chosen sustainability certification.
Empty pipes must have traction wire
Cable trays, lattice trays and cable ladders must be accessible for subsequent laying and replacement of cables and have at least 300 mm free space in front.
All sockets and connectors must be marked with the switchboard's number and group.

10.3.4. Electrical switchboards

Electrical switchboards
Electrical switchboards must be grey and made of metal.
Residual-current devices (RCD) must be of sufficient quality that they are not required to be inspected more frequently than every three years.
Electrical switchboards must be designed and placed so that they can be thermographed without interrupting the power supply.
Electrical switchboards must be thermographed at full load after commissioning.
All cables must be marked at terminations and penetrations.
There must be transparent doors on electrical panels so that fuses, etc. can be checked without opening the doors.
Fuse groups that do not need replacement of parts/components/fuses in the event of a failure are required.
It must be ensured that, if switchboards contain power cables and building automation, these must be visibly separated.
Additional meters must be installed, which enables the monitoring of energy consumption per floor, per shaft.
It must be possible for the energy consumption in the building to be monitored. It must be possible to separate process and comfort consumption from actual consumption. The following must be monitored by energy meters: servers, kitchen, refrigerator, ventilation, heating, special rooms.

10.3.5. General

General
Training of O&M staff must include instruction and review. Instruction must be an oral instruction in the use of the system in the various operating scenarios, maintenance procedures, troubleshooting, etc. The review must be a visual and practical instruction in the use of the system in the various operating scenarios, maintenance procedures, troubleshooting, etc. at the current facility if possible. If the instructor believes that it provides the greatest value to carry out both instruction and review at the same time, this must be submitted and approved by the Owner.

General
A training plan must be drawn up which contains at least: - Purpose of the training - Systems and facilities that are part of the training - Learning Objectives - Participants and teachers - Instructional equipment - Schedule - Assessment and follow-up
The training must contain the following learning topics: - Emergency situations - Normal operating situations - Maintenance Procedures - Maintenance of documentation
The training material must be handed in to the Owner for approval at least 10 days before the training takes place.
The training material must be submitted in open formats so that it can subsequently be updated and changed.
Interdisciplinary tests must be performed to verify the interaction of plants, installations and systems. All parties involved must actively participate in these tests.
Time must be set aside in the schedule for adjustments, tests and coordinated tests of the interaction of installations before delivery.
There must be a description of balancing methods in the project material.
All preconditions must be present for the balancing before it is carried out.
All balancing must be carried out and documented before delivery. Balancing and test plan must be approved by the Owner and the Cx Team.
Instruments used for measurement, regulation and setting must have valid calibration certificates.
The architect must ensure that there is room for a European pallet in strategic elevators, so that, for example, a pallet of A4 paper can be transported around.
Elevators must be prepared for access control both outside the elevator and inside it.

10.3.6. IT

IT
Ordinary cable ties must not be used to attach PDS cabling.
IT rooms (e.g. server rooms) may only contain IT related functions.

IT
Redundancy of IT infrastructure (components) must be determined: N, N + 1, 2N and approved by the Owner.
IT installations must be provided with no-break with at least 60 minutes of battery backup, so there is time for a controlled shutdown.
For connection of wireless LAN access points, data outlets must be established, so that it is possible to establish full coverage with wireless LAN throughout the building and on terraces in a grid with a double outlet per. 100 sqm.
There must be no foreign pipes, e.g., drains, sprinklers, water in IT rooms.
It must be ensured that there is good mobile coverage throughout the building and parking basement at all times when installing DAS systems.
It must be decided with the Owner whether DAS systems should be for several telecom operators.
There must be room to replace the base station of the DAS system.
Criteria for DAS systems must be established on the basis of the building's use and where personal densities are high.
IT installation must be tested cf. DS/EN 50346 annex I.

10.3.7. Cooling

Cooling
If there is more than one cooling machine, it must be possible to service one machine at a time without affecting the function or supply of components in production and distribution.
Solutions must allow the system to run at high efficiency at both full and partial loads.
Temperature settings on the cooling supply must be adjustable.
Natural refrigerants must be used.
There must be hydraulic separation of cooling production and distribution, using a buffer tank.
It must be possible to display the layers in the buffer tank graphically in the automation, as well as by thermometers on the buffer tank.
It must be possible to operate refrigeration plant without communication to the BMS system.
O&M staff must be able to monitor components of the cooling plant in real time.

Cooling
Energy meters must be installed so that a distinction can be made between consumption for comfort and for process.

10.3.8. Security

Security
The security systems must have full integration with both control and monitoring for the BMS system.
As a minimum, empty pipes must be established for all doors in concrete elements in preparation for the establishment of Access Control installations.
Natural smoke exhaust systems & powered smoke exhaust system: The system must be equipped with electric motors so that opening and closing can take place from operating pressure. Systems based on gas cartridges are not accepted.
Natural smoke exhaust systems & powered smoke exhaust system: Activation of replacement air vents must not compromise shell protection. Openings must not be accessible from the ground (at least 3 meters above the access platform).
Escape routes from non-access control areas must not pass through access control areas.
Building layout is designed so that guests do not have to go through more or less sensitive areas.
Automatic sliding doors and revolving doors must not be used as escape route doors to avoid requirements for automatic unlocking in connection with a possible fire alarm.
Security components must not be based on wireless communication; however, this does not apply to portable personal monitoring devices and control units.
Central control equipment for safety systems must be located in special rooms for this purpose, which are provided at the same time with electronic access control.
For specially secured areas, account must be taken of the fact that tailgating cannot be allowed.
The main entrance must be designed so that a lock function can be established so that the access control can be escalated in connection with special situations.
A "night box" must be set up so that regular suppliers can deliver goods without having to be locked in by staff.
Electrical and communication connections in the terrain must be secured against unauthorized intervention.
Fresh air intakes must be designed and located so that deliberate contamination of ventilation systems is prevented.

Security
Alert systems must be established as voice alarm systems.
Windows that are part of the shell protection must be provided with a relay switch function for closing and locking.
In connection with the selection of cameras for TVO, a physical demonstration with the current lighting must be established.
AIA control panel software must be able to handle a 25% expansion of connected components.
A PIR for AIA must be established at the entrance to floors, as well as possibly in front of stairs and lifts. Final extent must be clarified with the Owner.
It must be possible to automatically switch the AIA on and off in connection with access to special rooms.
There must be a UPS with 4 hours of battery backup for the IT network used for the security systems.

10.3.9. Solar shading

Solar shading
The solar shading must be controlled locally, understood in such a way that there must be sun and wind sensors on each facade section at least per module and it must be at two levels.
The control of the solar shading must take place via local control units connected in networks.
The solar shading control units must communicate the following with the BMS system: - Measured solar incidence (analog value) - Measured wind speed (analog value) - Setpoint sun exposure that triggers the shield (analog value) - Setpoint wind speed that forcibly opens the solar shading (analog value) - Alarm (digital value)

10.3.10. Ventilation

Ventilation
There must be a maximum CO_2 level of 750 ppm in the occupancy zone during normal working hours.
Fresh air intakes must be located so that they do not adversely affect air quality, e.g., from exhaust gases.

Ventilation
It must be possible to read the differential pressure across all filters in ventilation ducts.
During construction, all ducts and pipes must be sealed to cover against dirt and dust.
It must be ensured that there can be no short-circuiting of air between the kitchen and comfort ventilation.
It must be possible to regulate meeting rooms and/or other living areas individually.
It must be possible to organize periodic inspections of fire dampers so that they do not interfere with the employees' daily work.
It must be possible to service ventilation fire dampers without the use of mechanical aids.
Ventilation fire dampers must be set up so that they can be replaced without destructive work.
Handles, measuring points and unloading points, including pressure and temperature, etc., must be positioned so that O&M staff can access them without aids (e.g., ladder). They must be located at least 110 cm above the floor and a maximum of 190 cm above the floor.

10.3.11. Plumbing systems

Plumbing systems
It must be possible to measure differential pressure over dirt collectors, partial flow filters, pumps, exchangers, ventilation surfaces, fan coils, heating blankets, motor valves and non-return valves.
Installations must be adjusted with a measurement tolerance of +/- 5% percent.
A balancing report must be prepared, stating which errors have been located in connection with the adjustment. The balancing report must be submitted to the Cx Team for approval before commissioning.
After balancing, all valves and pumps must be fitted with balancing labels and locked. The labels must be laminated so that they have the same lifetime as the components they are on.
For all control valves and differential pressure regulators, the label must state the KVS value of the valves and the pressure class of the differential pressure regulators.
Pumps must be dimensioned so that they have sufficient capacity to regulate in proportional pressure.
Shut-off valves must be accessible without the need for destructive work/alterations.

Plumbing systems
Handles, measuring points and unloading points must be located so that the operation can access them without aids (e.g.. ladder).
Liquid samples must be taken 6 months after commissioning and sent for analysis.
A filter plan must be prepared which describes which filter sizes are used in the installation during commissioning and in the future.
It must be ensured that, before commissioning of the system, the necessary cleaning is carried out by flushing, so that impurities which have been added to the system during construction and which may cause operational disturbances are removed. Larger distribution lines and the like are flushed through. The system is flushed with full pump pressure and open valves until dirt is no longer collected in the filters.
A flushing plan must be drawn up to ensure that all parts of the installation are cleaned before commissioning.
It must be possible to vent the system with vacuum vents on both the primary and secondary side of all systems.
The use of hot water circulation must be minimized with regard to energy consumption, tapping points and bacterial growth. Heat loss in the circulation line must be calculated.
It must be possible to read the differential pressure across filters on all water-bearing systems.
Water-bearing systems must be designed in such a way that it is possible to create a hydraulic balance in zones so that parts of the system can be adjusted without disturbing the rest of the building. The zoning must be at least per floor.
Water traps must be located so that the operation has sufficient access to their maintenance.
It must be possible to clear dirt collectors on the system without major spillage of liquids.
Dirt collectors from dimension DN65 and upwards must be made with a valve so that water can be drained off.
There must be the possibility of shut-off on both sides of filters, dirt collectors and pumps.
There must be labels on the dirt collector and partial flow filter, stating when they were last cleaned and the size of the filter.
It must be possible for the person filling the water to monitor the static pressure in the installation from the filling point while the water is filling.
Leakage measurements must be installed in strategic locations in the distribution system.
Consumption measurements must be made of all media at floor level and sectioned based on branches (e.g., per technical shaft).

10.4. Table of Contents of the Commissioning Plan

Example of a Cx Plan's table of contents.

1. General

1.1. Content of the Cx Plan
1.2. Scope of the Cx Process
1.3. Structure of the Cx Plan

2. Organization

2.1. Management of the process
2.2. Possible impartiality
2.3. Contracts and agreements
2.4. Responsiblity matrix

3. Pre-Design

3.1. Organization
3.2. Owner's Project Requirements
3.3. The Cx Plan
3.4. Specify the participation of the Design Team
3.5. Cx Log
3.6. Cx Design Review
3.7. Phase acceptance

4. Design Development

4.1. Start-up meetig
4.2. Basis of Design
4.3. Documentation requirements, Systems Manual
4.4. Cx Design Review
4.5. Phase acceptance

5. Construction documents

5.1. Specify the participation of the Contractor
5.2. Site Inspection plans
5.3. Test overview
5.5. Test schedule
5.5. Cx Design Review
5.6. Updating of the Cx Plan
5.7. Updating of the Cx Log
5.8. Phase acceptrance

6. Construction phase

6.1. Training plan for the O&M staff
6.2. Perfoming Site Inspections
6.3. Additional Cx Design Review
6.4. Test paradigms
6.5. Test overview
6.6. Executing tests
6.7. Training the O&M staff
6.8. Review of the Contractors quality assurance
6.9. Systems Manual
6.10. Updating Cx documents
6.11. Cx Report
6.12. Phase acceptance

7. Occupancy and Operations phase

7.1. Stress tests
7.2. Seasonal tests
7.3. 10 months inspection
7.4. Updating the Cx documents
7.5. Phase acceptrance

10.5. Training plan with examples of learning objectives

The example below contains training objectives and general information. The training objectives must be adapted to the specific facility and installations.

Learning Objectives
Operation 1) Normal operating situation 2) Abnormal operating situation 3) Testing after service
Maintenance 1) Own service 2) Service via contracts 3) Tests after service
Troubleshooting 1) Steps to isolate the fault 2) Contact data for key people from supplier
Emergency 1) Procedure to stop the emergency 2) Contact data for key people
General maintenance 1) Instructions for filter change 2) Instructions for heat exchanger 3) Checking the fire thermostat 4) Control and testing of the frost protection 5) Instructions for replacing sensors 6) Review of the principle of placement of dampers 7) Guidance in where the damper appears on drawings 8) Review of hidden locations

Information & Schedule
A practical review of all the learning objectives is carried out. The practical instruction and theoretical review are carried out if possible at the same time and it is carried out at the current plant. Scheduling and time periods for the teaching are stated in the schedule: TX_ZX-001

Material used in education:
As-Built documentation, operating instructions and test paradigms are used in connection with the teaching.

Material handed out:
The following information is provided on USB after the lesson: As-Built documentation, operating instructions, test paradigms and pictures of the plant.

10.6. Test paradigm (indoor climate test)

Name of test	Indoor climate test in a summer season
System name	VA13_TRx01
System type	Indoor climate
Test data	2021-02-01
Test leader	Thomas T. Jarløv
Participants	John Jensen, Company1, BMS Ole Olsen, Company2, Ventilation

Purpose of test

The purpose of the test is to demonstrate that temperature and air speed requirements for the indoor climate are complied with and that the system has a stable regulation. The test must verify that the plats operate as a single system.	OPR items, reference: - ID 113 - ID 114 - ID 117

Prerequisites for the test

ID	Prerequisites	OK/FAIL
1	BMS, electricity, cooling, heating and ventilation are mechanically complete, cf. the test overview.	
2	Balancing reports have been approved by the construction management and the Cx team.	
3	Quality assurance documentation is available for all subject areas.	
4	Maintenance plans and documentation have been submitted for all components.	
5	Approved pre-test report.	

Instruments and equipment used during the test

Purpose	Product name	Calibration date
Air speedometer	SWEMA 3000	2021-01-10
CO2 and pressure gauge	Testo 160 IAQ	2021-01-20
Temperature and moisture meter	Testo 176-H1	2021-01-20

Risks and consequential damages

Risk/consequential damages	Mitigating action
During the test, malfunctions may occur due to manual override of pumps and valves.	The Owner's O&M organization must be continuously informed when manual overrides are made.

Test procedure

Info:
The indoor climate test is performed as a specific test of one office, as well as a general verification of the entire system, consisting of BMS, electricity, cooling, heating and ventilation.

The test is performed over a 20-day summer period, where logging of all parameters on the system is performed continuously, with logging of temperature, humidity, CO2 and air velocities in the specific areas.

During the test, controlled step responses are performed, which must document the system's control stability.

Test setup and logging:

ID	Procedure	OK/FAIL	Result
1	General lighting: 8 W/m2 Special lighting: 4 pieces/20W Total electronics: 200W Persons: 4 persons (1.2 met) Simultaneity factor: 0.9		
2	Logging equipment is set up according to locations specified in appendix "Floor plan of equipment".		
3	All logging parameters according to the BMS functional description are active and the logging period is set to 2 years.		

Temperature requirements:

ID	Procedure	OK/FAIL	Result
1	The vertical temperature difference must not exceed 2°C and be measured at a height of 1.1 m and 0.1 m above the floor.		
2	The temperature should be between 21-22°C.		

Air speed:

ID	Procedure	OK/FAIL	Result
1	The air speed must be less than 0.22m/s. 5 observations of 30 minutes are made over the test, where the test leader ensures that there is no influence on the test instrument (e.g., by persons going by).		

Step-response:

ID	Procedure	OK/FAIL	Result
1	2 step responses are performed on the 8th and 14th test day with an increase and decrease of respectively 3°C and 5°C. The control stability must comply with the requirements in accordance with the functional description.		

Conclusion

The test is approved / not approved.

Notes:

Appendix

System structure of main system:

Floorplan with indication of where temperature loggers are located:

10.7. Test requirements

This appendix contains examples from Copenhagen Airports test requirements for selected installations.

10.7.1. Automatic fire alarm

Automatic Fire Alarm System detects fire.

Topic	Test
Test	Spot testing of detectors and groups.
Test	Testing of the entire signal path with test report.
Test	Testing of detector, e.g., with smoke/gas and signal to cabinet.
Documentation	O-plans (As a minimum redlines O-plans).
Documentation	Operating log is available at the fire alarm control panel, cf. DBI 232.
Documentation	O&M documentation is available at the fire alarm control panel, cf. DBI 232.
Documentation	System Matrix must be available. All systems with affiliation, system names and functions affected by Automatic Fire Alarm System must be specified.
Documentation	For more than x > 600m^2, a remark-free inspection report must be submitted to the authorities.
Documentation	For smaller x < 600m^2, it must be reported to DBI.
Documentation	O&M plan has been submitted to the project's Cx Provider.
SIT	System integration test cf. DBI RL 006. (For interconnected installations, system integration tests must be performed).

10.7.2. Power-Operated Fire Doors

Power-Operated Fire Doors are doors that normally are opened and closed electrically or pneumatically.

Topic	Test
Visual	The door operating pressure (manual closing pressure) is set up next to the door and activates controller.

Topic	Test
Visual	The door operating pressure is marked with an engraved sign indicating "Close door".
Visual	The electrical controller is marked door number.
Visual	Fire-/smoke detectors must be marked with "POFD" (yellow sign with black writing).
Test	Function test of the fire-/smoke detectors with test smoke or gas. This must activate the electrical controller.
Test	Function test with test button on electrical controller.
Test	Function test with the door operating pressure.
Test	The door(s) closes completely in folds.
Test	For multi-wing doors, the door selector must ensure that the doors close in the correct order.
Test	The door closes when disconnecting power supply.
SIT	When activating electrical controller, any door-automation is switched off/overridden so that it does not work until electrical controller's fault/alarm has been reset. "Door-automation" includes both the door's own automation and any PLC control.
SIT	At doors in passenger-flow areas, an alarm must be issued to the control center when the electrical controller is activated.
SIT	Possible emergency power supply/battery backup has been tested. The supply to the electrical controller is interrupted and a wait of X minutes before the test is performed.
Documentation	Function test report cf. "Appendix 1" in DBI Guideline 231.
Documentation	O&M plan has been submitted to the project's Cx Provider.

10.7.3. Automatic Warning System

Automatic Warning System is used for warning.

Topic	Test
Visual	The installation is a secure network installation.
Test	The system can be manually activated from the operational center.
Test	The IT installations are monitored. Fault detection is tested when disconnecting the IT connection.

Topic	Test
Test	Full scale test required by the authorities (including associated functions, e.g., music)
Test	STIPA and sound pressure measurement.
SIT	Pre-test (including transmission of signals to the BMS, music override, etc.). All errors and signal output must be transmitted to the BMS system.
Documentation	O&M documentation.
Documentation	Commissioning report.
Documentation	Functional test report.
Documentation	DBI remark-free inspection report.
Documentation	STIPA and sound pressure measurements. Measurement results must comply with DBI R024.
Documentation	Floor plans and diagrams with all connections.
Documentation	O&M plan has been submitted to the project's Cx Provider.

10.7.4. Lighting system

Lighting systems and associated BMS control.

Topic	Test
Visual	The control switch in the switchboard must have the positions engraved, cf. OPR.
Measurement	Lighting measurement (Control test & measurement of lux, RA and Kelvin)
Test	Functional test cf. BR § 384 (Functional test & measurement of lux, RA and Kelvin)
Test	The relays in the switchboard are tested for all locations. The corresponding lamps are checked.
Test	Switch-off function cf. OPR must be tested. - The voltage is interrupted and light reacts cf. OPR.

Topic	Test
SIT	Pre-test for lighting installations with BMS monitoring. - The lighting is switched on and the BMS screens symbolizes the areas that are lit. - The lighting must be able to be switched on and off through the BMS. - When the controlling BMS sub-switchboard is switched off and the light is switched on for the area. - Setpoint for the lux requirements is changed and the light switches on/off. - Time program in the BMS is reviewed.
Documentation	Measurement report on lux, RA and Kelvin.
Documentation	Function test report cf. BR § 384 (Measurement report for lux, RA and Kelvin, control, zones, daylight).
Documentation	Luminaire plan (omitted, e.g., in technical rooms).
Documentation	O&M plan has been submitted to the project's Cx Provider.

10.7.5. Doors with automation

Doors with automatic can be sliding doors, revolving doors, etc.

Topic	Test
Visual	The automation is sufficiently mounted and fastened and in good condition.
Visual	It must be possible for one man to take off any coat for servicing. It must be possible to remove the coat, i.e., there must be no wire attached to it.
Visual	There must be no self-tapping screws that could damage the operating personnel during servicing.
Test	Self-learning/calibration has been performed, so endpoints, speed, etc., is set.
Test	The door pressure is checked.
Test	All sensors connected have been tested individually and the function is in accordance with the description.
Test	Functional test.
Test	The supply is disconnected and reconnected. It must be verified that there is an automatic restart after a power failure.
Test	Any emergency pressure releases the door.

Topic	Test
Test	The door(s) closes completely in folds (fariles)
Test	For multi-wing doors, the door selector must ensure that the doors close in the correct order.
SIT	If the door is connected to a PLC control, e.g. at gates and aerial bridges, this control integration must be tested. The PLC control is tested, the door control is tested and then the controls are tested in interaction.
SIT	Alarm transmission to the operation central with activation of camera and possible siren (All transmission options, e.g. emergency pressure, magnet, etc.)
Safety	Final inspection cf. the *Machinery Directive* has been performed and approved.
Documentation	Functional test report cf.
Documentation	O&M plan has been submitted to the project's Cx Provider.

10.7.6. Elevators

Testing of elevators. This test is an addition to the 3rd party inspection and is performed by the Cx Team.

Topic	Test
Visual	The chair and group have been cleaned.
Visual	Visual check that all signs and markings are intact
Visual	Visual check that the rescue space in the shaft bottom is marked.
Visual	There must be pictograms on screen at alarm press.
Test	Test runs have been performed from all floors.
Test	Test of emergency lighting in the chair. The supply is interrupted and the emergency lighting is activated.
Test	All LED's in pushbuttons light up when activated on each floor.
Test	Testing of communication and alarm systems. Calls are made from chair to operation central and sound and speech level are checked. It should be a silent background call.

Topic	Test
Test	Testing of the safety functions of all floor and chair doors is effective, e.g.: - 3D light carpets - Closing pressure - The distance between doors is max 4 mm
Test	All door locks and other security items are reviewed. - The door locks on each floor are checked with a special key. - When the door to the lower floor is opened via a special key, it must be ensured that the safety pawl must be reset manually.
Test	Testing of fitter driving can be done during inspection from both top and bottom. Test driving must check that the chair can run both up and down.
Test	Test of emergency lighting on chair top. The supply is interrupted and emergency lighting is activated.
Test	The chair can be overridden via control panel/HMI. Test drive is performed.
Test	Functional test cf. BR § 249 must document the elevator's energy consumption
Security	Inspection of the 3rd party report.
SIT	If there is an access control on the lift, this must be tested with the Owner's access card.
SIT	The full signal path for the Automatic Fire Alarm System must be tested. It is not enough just to make a termination in the elevator board. A fire signal is made from Fire Alarm Control Panel: - The elevator responds according to the fire strategy and runs to the specified floor. - The elevator cannot be used after activation. - For firefighter elevators, test the function.
Documentation	The O&M documentation is accessible on the wall or top of the lift.
Documentation	Approved report from inspection body (3rd party)
Documentation	Function test report cf. BR § 249 must document the elevator's energy consumption
Documentation	O&M plan has been submitted to CPH's Cx Provider, including specifications, cf. Executive Order 461, section 25, subsection. 2.

10.7.7. Cooling system

Cooling systems can be small decentralized systems or large central systems.

The example below must be expanded with the OPR requirements.

Topic	Test
Visual	The location of components corresponds to their location on the diagram.
Test	Pressure tests have been performed.
Test	Adjustment cf. DS 469 & OPR.
Test	Noise measurement is performed if applicable.
Test	Checking the connection of room thermostats with the rooms.
Test	Checking safety precautions.
Test	Control of thermal indoor climate.
Test	Functional test documenting that the system complies with BR's requirements for balancing and control, cf. BR § 391
Test	Load test - the system is run and it is confirmed that it can deliver the designed power.
Security	3rd party approval has been performed with satisfactory result.
Safety	Final inspection cf. the *Machinery Directive* has been performed and approved.
SIT	Pre-test where all functions are tested across contract boundaries. - All signals to the BMS signal must be tested - All forms of management, cf. function description, have been tested
Documentation	Balancing report cf. DS 469 & the Cx template.
Documentation	Functional test report documenting that the system complies with BR's requirements for balancing and control, cf. BR § 391.
Documentation	O&M plan has been submitted to the project's Cx Provider.

10.7.8. Powered Smoke Exhaust System

Powered Smoke Exhaust Systems are used to remove cold smoke mechanically, e.g., by fans.

Topic	Test
Visual	If supply separators are fitted in front of fans, confirm compliance with the fire strategy.

Topic	Test
Visual	The BMS screens must state the zone name and fire pressure ID for the fire pressures that activate the system.
Test	Functional test.
Test	Balancing of air volumes + measurement.
Test	The system is forced into fault and it is verified that the fault signal is transmitted to the BMS system. Errors must be checked: - Remove hose from pressure switch - Disconnection of supply separators for fans If faults are only detected during weekly tests, weekly tests are performed via the BMS when faults are forced.
Test	Weekly tests are activated on the system via the BMS. The system must perform a full weekly test and the performed weekly test must be logged in the BMS system.
Test	The system is started by activating fire pressure - all fire pressures must be tested.
SIT	Pre-test where all functions are tested across contract boundaries. This includes checking BMS signals. (Functions, controls and signals across professional and contract boundaries are tested)
Safety	Final inspection cf. the *Machinery Directive* has been performed and approved.
Documentation	TAB report.
Documentation	Operating instructions describing the function of the system, including which supply air openings must be open. The instructions must be visible and attached to the system's control panel. The guide must also be submitted as part of the O&M documentation. Instructions must include: - Visual display of zones with indication of zone name - Visual display of where fire pressure is located with their fire pressure ID numbers - Visual display of where fans are located, with their system name (often BMS address)
Documentation	O&M plan has been submitted to the project's Cx Provider.

10.7.9. Emergency Lighting System

The Emergency Lighting System must ensure a lux level on surfaces in the event that the general lighting is not present.

Topic	Test
Visual	Luminaire plan is compared with current marking, programming and in the switchboard.
Test	Checking the emergency operation of the safety lighting in the event of a main power supply failure. Has been tested and is in operation after 60 minutes, cf. DBI guide 34 appendix 7.5
Test	Checking the panic lighting gives a lighting level of at least 1.0 lux after 60 minutes of emergency operation with other lighting switched off, cf. DBI guide 34 appendix 7.5
Test	Checking the emergency operation of the safety lighting in the event of a main power supply failure at the individual light groups (selective switching on of the safety lighting), cf. DBI guide 34 appendix 7.5
Test	A check has been made that the addresses of all luminaires correspond to marking, programming in the Emergency Lighting System control panel and the associated floor plan.
Test	Test cf. DBI guide 34 must be expected to be carried out as night work. (The Contractor is responsible for coordination with operational center and security).
SIT	Pre-test where all functions are tested across contract boundaries. If the control panel is connected to BMS or if the control panel is connected to IT monitoring, all signals must be checked.
Documentation	Test report cf. DBI guide 34 appendix 7.5.
Documentation	Floor plan with indication of the addresses of all luminaires.
Documentation	O&M plan has been submitted to the project's Cx Provider.

10.7.10. Automatic Opening Vent (natural smoke ventilation)

The Automatic Opening Vent ventilates cold smoke via natural ventilation.

Topic	Test
Visual	Print is marked with fire pressure ID number
Visual	Operating pressure is located at the control panel which opens. This means that there is both fire pressure and a pressure at the control panel.
Visual	There is a power supply separator in front of the motor.

Topic	Test
Test	All signals to the BMS must be tested. It includes feedback and error signals.
Test	The operating press opens the window.
Test	Check that the control panel does not go into comfort mode (blue diode).
Safety	Final inspection cf. the *Machinery Directive* has been performed and approved.
SIT	Pre-test where all functions are tested across contract boundaries.
Documentation	O&M plan has been submitted to the project's Cx Provider.

10.8. Fire technical system integration test

A full scale SIT test must be performed on the building's fire-fighting installations. Where several fire-fighting installations are to work together, a system integration test must be carried out before the building is put into operation, which shows that the coherent system of installations has the desired function.

Before the system integration test can be performed, the following documentation must be approved:

a. Control matrix (how the different fire technical installations are connected)
b. System documentation
c. QA documentation

The following must participate in the system integration test:

a. The Cx Team
b. The Fire technical specialist
c. The Contractors from the various fire-fighting installations

The test must include the following plant types if the project contains them:

a. Automatic Fire Alarm System
b. Automatic system for closing of fireproof doors
c. Automatic Fire Sprinkler System
d. Acoustic Warning System
e. Automatic fire ventilation
f. Automatic Gas Extinguishing System
g. Firefighter elevators
h. Firefighter panels
i. Fire dampers
j. Elevators

k. Release of locks on escape routes

l. Escalators

m. Safety lighting

Figure 29 shows how a building's fire-fighting installations can react when a fire is detected. When the fire occurs, smoke and heat will be detected and/or the sprinkler system will be activated. This will cause the Automatic Fire Alarm System to alert the emergency services, as well as initiate the activities specified in the control matrix defined in the building's fire strategy, such as stopping comfort ventilation, closing fireproof doors, etc.

The area marked in gray shows that the Automatic Fire Alarm System sends a stop signal to 3 different systems: ventilation, escalators and elevators. Most often, it is different Contractors who carry out the Automatic Fire Alarm System installation and the interconnected systems. Therefore, the interfaces, which consist of a signal transmission and associated function, must be tested. All possible fire scenarios must be tested and it must be verified that all installations respond correctly.

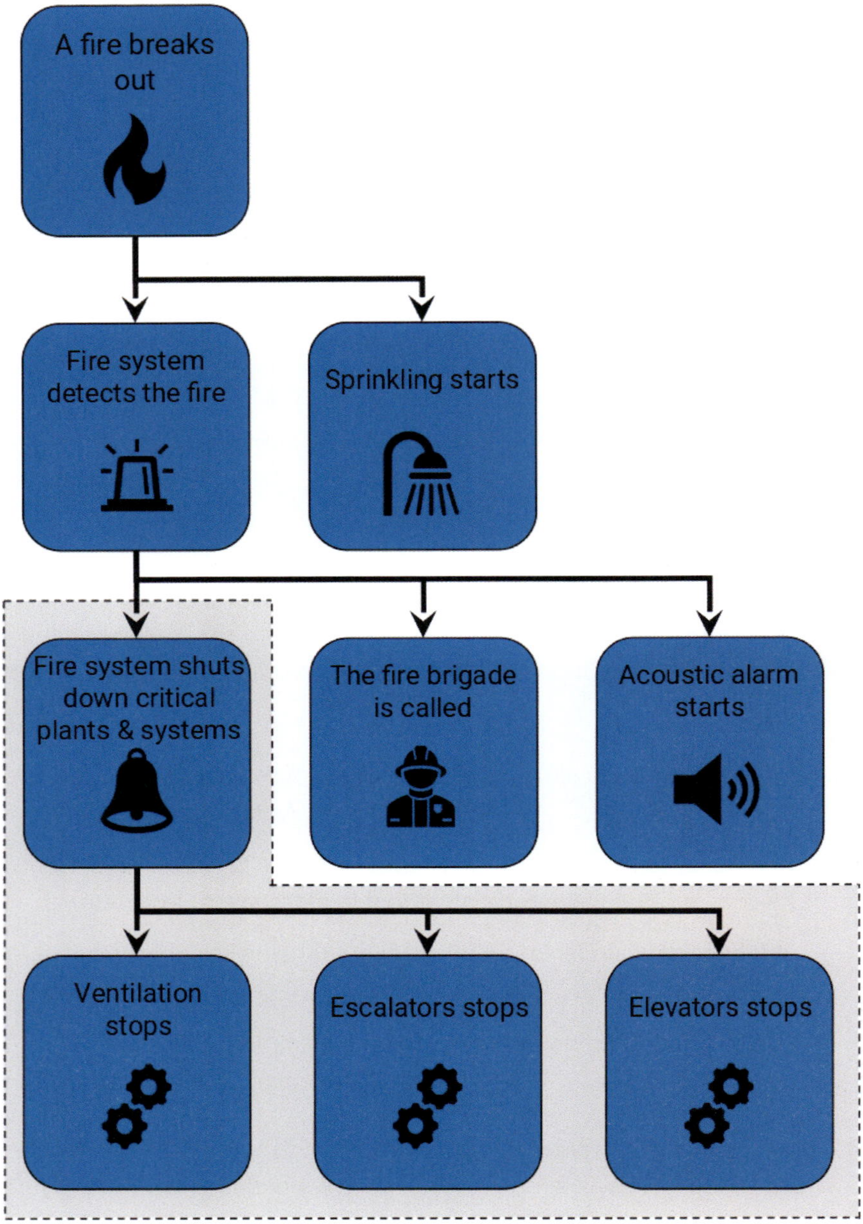

Figure 29. Example of the integrations in the Automatic Fire Alarm System

10.9. Description: Pre-test

"Pre-test" is considered an ordinary part of the Contractor's quality assurance that the delivered project meets the project requirements. The pre-test is a verification that plants, installations and systems operate across disciplines and contract boundaries, as described in the project material.

If the project material prescribes a function that connects two works/functions/systems together, e.g., that a signal from system A causes a mechanical reaction in system B, the pre-test must document that the performed solution works across these systems.

In the case of BMS-connected installations and facilities, the pre-test must be managed by the BMS Contractor, but the turnkey Contractor/main Contractor is responsible for the test, including convening and coordination with the Contractors from the other disciplines. The Contractors disciplines other than the BMS must assist the BMS Contractor in the pre-test of the system.

If the installation or system has no interaction or connection with other disciplines and works, the pre-test is covered by the normal testing, which must demonstrate that the function works in accordance with the project requirements.

Normally, the Cx Provider would not participate in the pre-test. However, there must be an opportunity for the Cx Provider to participate.

Documentation of the completed and successful pre-test is a prerequisite for conducting the final Cx test.

10.10. Description: Cx test

The Cx test is the final verification of the OPR. The Cx test is a counterpart to the pre-test, which means that if the pre-test is performed and approved, the Cx test should not find any errors.

The Contractors for the disciplines involved in the Cx test are responsible for participating in and performing the test procedures specified and managed by the Cx Provider.

The Cx test has two primary purposes:

a. Verification that the pre-test has been performed correctly

b. All operating scenarios have been tested.

c. Operational introduction for the Owner's O&M staff, so that the staff has knowledge of and has tested all functions, cf. the project requirements, before the project is taken into operation.

The test procedure for the Cx test varies depending on the subject area being tested. As a starting point, the same procedure is used, but with the exclusion of irrelevant areas:

a. Visual check (design elements, tolerances, cable markings, availability, operating options, etc.)

b. Checking/testing of safety elements (gas detectors, emergency ventilation, fire and frost thermostats, safety switches, etc.)

c. Control/testing of functions (signals, mechanical reactions and the sequence of these, etc.)

d. Control/test of operating scenarios (different operating scenarios and conditions, partial load, full load, etc.)

The Cx Provider is responsible for the execution of the Cx test. The Contractors responsible for the installations must attend in order to clarify questions.

10.11. Questionnaire for lessons learned

The table below shows an excerpt from a survey conducted at Copenhagen Airports. The questionnaire is only a subjective assessment and must be expanded with the option for the participants to also give specific suggestions for improvements. The Cx Organization, the project managers and the O&M staff participated.
The study was not anonymous in this case, as there was a desire to be able to contact the participants afterwards to have the evaluation elaborated.

The answers were ranked from 0-5 with the following definition:

- 0 - I don't know
- 1 - Strongly disagree
- 2 - Disagree
- 3 - Neutral
- 4 - Agree
- 5 - Strongly agree

Topic: Resource-involvement and -management	Answers (0-5)
Cx has contributed to an optimized resource involvement.	
Cx has ensured that only the right/needed persons participated in verification activities.	
It has been a help that Cx has acted as a "single-point-of-contact" for the O&M staff.	
Cx must continue to help with resource management.	

Topic: Coordination and management of test activities.	Answers (0-5)
Cx has helped with fewer wasted hours during testing (e.g., fewer re-tests).	
Cx has improved the test process for all participants.	
Cx has helped to increase transparency in what and when to test.	
Cx must continue to help with managing the testing activities.	

Subject: More efficient handover.	**Answers (0-5)**
Cx helps to set a uniformed framework for the handover process.	
Cx has helped with the transition from project to operation.	
Cx must continue to assist with the handover process.	

11. References

- AABC Commissioning Group (2005), ACG Commissioning Guideline.
- ASHRAE (2007), ASHRAE Guideline 1.1-2007 - HVAC&R Technical Requirements for the Commissioning Process.
- ASHRAE (2018), ASHRAE Standard 202 - Commissioning Process for Buildings and Systems.
- ASHRAE (2019), ASHRAE Guideline 0 - The Commissioning Process.
- California Commissioning Collaborative (2006), California Commissioning Guide: Existing Buildings.
- California Commissioning Collaborative (2006), California Commissioning Guide: New Buildings.
- CxPlanner.com (2021), CxPlanner - online Cx software.
- CxWiki.dk (2021), CxWiki - online Danish commissioning wikipedia.
- Dansk Standard (2014), DS 3090 - Commissioning process for buildings - Installations in new buildings and major conversions (Danish).
- DBI (2021), The Danish Institute of Fire and Security Technology
- DTU (2010), Building Commissioning: Advantages and disadvantages of the process and how it has been applied in Denmark.
- Energy Design Resources (2010), Building Commissioning Guidelines.
- Evan Mills (2009), A Golden Opportunity for Reducing Energy Costs and Greenhouse Gas Emissions.
- International Code Council (2018), ICC G4-2018 Guideline for Commissioning.
- Lawrence Berkeley National Laboratory (2018), Commissioning Cost/Benefit Study Findings.
- NIBS (2012), NIBS Guideline 3-2012 - Building Enclosure Commissioning Process BECx.
- The Building Commissioning Association (2011), New Construction Building Commissioning Best Practice.
- The International Energy Agency (2010), EBC Annex 47 - Commissioning

Process for Buildings and Systems.

- TTJ.dk (2021), Blog about commissioning.
- U.S. Department of Energy (2014), Commissioning for Federal Facilities.
- Værdibyg (2013), Commissioning-processen.

Printed in Poland
by Amazon Fulfillment
Poland Sp. z o.o., Wrocław
04 August 2023

e228809d-5146-4773-9480-449ce1e574f7R01